Jamestown REDISCOVERY VII

W9-BXN-239

William M. Kelso
  J. Eric Deetz
    Seth W. Mallios
      Beverly A. Straube

The Association for the Preservation
of Virginia Antiquities
2001

Dedicated to the memory of our dear friends and colleagues!

Dr. James "Jim" Deetz: Scholar, Mentor, Jamestown Rediscovery Advisor, and Friend.

Harvey Patterson: Inspirator, Veteran, Jamestown Rediscovery Volunteer, and Friend.

Graphics by Jamie E. May

Design and production by David M. Givens

Printed in The United States of America

ISBN: 0-917565-11-8

PREFACE

Jamestown Rediscovery VII is the seventh booklet in a series of yearly updates on the historical and archaeological research known as *Jamestown Rediscovery,* carried out under the auspices of the Association for the Preservation of Virginia Antiquities on its 22.5 acres on Jamestown Island. From
the outset, there were two major goals for the project: (1) find, uncover,
and recover whatever might remain of the earliest settlement and the growth
of the 17th-century town *and,* at the same time, (2) make that process of
discovery as accessible to the visiting public as possible. For that reason the
site and related laboratory work is as visitor friendly as it can be, and considerable staff effort has gone into publishing the results of the research in a
timely manner. Part of that publishing program is the *Rediscovery* series,
which is literally rushed into print before the excitement of discovery fades.
The down side of such a rapid publication program is that the time for full
analysis to support conclusions is constricted, and therefore the meaning of
discoveries is always subject to change through time. Therefore the reader
should be advised that what appears in print every year is not necessarily a
conclusion but rather *a working theory* to be tested during future research.
That, of course, is not really any different then any attempt to reconstruct
and understand the past. However, the yearly deadline here distills the process and renders most attempts to breath meaning into the discoveries all
the more tentative.

The Rediscovery Project was conceived to be a ten-year effort, 1994-2003,
culminating in the production of both a comprehensive publication of the
results of the research and a popular-level account of the historical background and APVA archaeological discoveries both by 2005-2006. Along
the way, periodical articles were planned as part of each year's work. In reality, the "articles" instantly grew into the more comprehensive yearly
Jamestown Rediscovery booklets which were time-consuming in-house pro-
ductions. This resulted nonetheless, in time well invested in that each edition required archaeological and documentary background research that will
ultimately prove useful in final interpretive works. At this point in time
however, future publication must be focused on more comprehensive manu-
scripts so that they can be published in time for the 400th anniversary of
the founding of Jamestown, 2007. Consequently, the *Jamestown Rediscovery* series will end with this volume to be replaced by annual updates for
inclusions in an APVA newsletter.

Acknowledgements:

The achievements of Jamestown Rediscovery are due in large measure
to the many individuals and organizations who have provided leader-
ship, generous financial support and scholarly advice and expertise.

Among the hundreds who could be acknowledged, we highlight a few here for special recognition:

Jamestown Rediscovery national Advisory Board: Dr. Warren M. Billings, chairman, Dennis B. Blanton, Dr. Edward Bond, Frederick Faust, Dr. Jeffrey P. Brain, Dr. Cary Carson, Dr. Kathleen Deagan, Dr. Rex M. Ellis, Dr. Alaric Faulkner, Dr. William W. Fitzhugh, , Ms. Camille Hedrick, Dr. James Horn, Dr. Jon Kukla, Dr. Douglas Owsley, Dr. David Orr, Mr. Oliver Perry, Dr. Carmel Schrire, Dr. George Stuart, Dr. Sandra Treadway, Dr. Edwin Randolph Turner, Mr. Robert Wharton

Roxane Gilmore, First Lady of Virginia

APVA's Trustees, staff and membership for their constant interest and support

Our colleagues at the National Park Service, Colonial National Historical Park and the National Park Foundation

Generous Benefactors include: The United States Congress, The Commonwealth of Virginia, National Geographic Society, National Endowment for the Humanities, James City County, The Mary Morton Parsons Foundation, Jessie Ball duPont Fund, William Byrd Branch of the APVA, the Beirne Carter Foundation, the Eugene Holt Foundation, Mr. and Mrs. William M. Grover, Jr., Mr. and Mrs. John A. Prince, Alan M. Voorhees, Mr. and Mrs. T. Eugene Worrell, Mr. and Mrs. Martin Kirwan King, and The Mrs. Mattielene T. King Estate. And Patricia Cornwell for underwriting special needs such as the annual field school, research travel, technical equipment and forensic anthropological research.

Staff: The Rediscovery Project has been very much a team effort from the start and now very much an experienced team effort. With an open mind to ways of improving the process, over the initial six years of the project, the staff has had the opportunity to ever fine tune the way things have been done. I am especially grateful for their ability to together decipher the ever-widening archaeological story of Jamestown. I am indebted to curator Bly Straube's superior and ever-growing understanding of post-medieval material culture; field supervisor Eric Deetz's growing insight into post-medieval vernacular architecture and his unique ability to educate visitors; graphic artist/archaeologist Jamie May's superior eye for beauty on the computer and for reading the archaeological signs of Jamestown's first burials and last statehouse; field supervisor Seth Mallios for his tremendous research energy and great teaching talent; Ashley McKeown for her insight and ability to unravel the art and mystery of Jamestown's skeletal biology; conservator/photographer Michael Lavin's ever more uniquely experienced conservation touches and photographic eye; and for office manager/

research assistant Catherine Correll-Wall's talent for so delicately balancing the ever-more complicated project schedule and at the same time seeking out a fresh Jamestown documentary story.

2000 Stalwart Crew: Tonia Rock, Shane Emmett, Daniel Gamble, Adam Heinrich, Carter C. Hudgins, Heather Lapham, Ernelyn Marx, Daniel Schmidt, Sarah Stroud.

2000 Field School Participants: Kara Bartels, Mike Bienstock, Lucia Boatman, Karen Gauthier, Roxane Gilmore, Lisa Gijanto, Brian Gohacki, Tom Goyne Jamie Helmick, Michelle Hinton, Cary Hudgins, Kirk Kehrberg, Teresa Moyer, Jennifer Podolsky, Stephen Putnam, Amber Rhodes, Donald Sadler, Flora Slater, Will Tatum, Whitney Thomey, Nila Varma, Alyssa Wyklige.

The Corps of APVA interpreters.

Paula Neely for editing.

For me, Ellen, my ever suffering proofreader, makes this all worthwhile.

WMK, Jamestown, Virginia 7/27/01.

™

CHAPTER 1 — by William M. Kelso

Discoveries 2000

From its beginning in 1994, the major goal of the Association for the Preservation of Virginia Antiquities' Jamestown Rediscovery excavations was to locate and uncover any remains of the first Jamestown settlement, especially traces of the original James Fort and other phases of the fort's evolving design during the Virginia Company years, 1607 to 1624.[1]

When the project began, it was commonly believed that the Fort was long gone. Various visitors to Jamestown Island since 1842, and archaeologists who had tested the Association for the Preservation of Virginia Antiquities' (APVA) property, thought that all traces of the James Fort settlement had been lost through erosion of the James River shoreline.[2] To the contrary, evidence from the first five seasons of digging now clearly indicates that the archaeological remains of the early settlement do still exist on the APVA property. In fact, archaeolgists estimate that about 85 percent of the original Fort site is still above water.

Figure 1. James Fort excavation plan.

Remains of James Fort

Archaeologists uncovered the southeastern corner of the Fort during 1994 to 1999.[3] That discovery included slot trenches where upright side-by-side log palisades and a curved dry moat once stood. Other signs included two "pits" or cellars inside the palisade lines; one near the southeast corner and another amid the curve of the Fort's corner bulwark, possibly a secondary powder magazine. Both these and the Fort moat had been filled in with mixed clay transported there from some other original colonial excavation and with rich deposits of discarded armor, pottery, copper, waste from making glass and garbage bones from the 1607 to 1610 period.

Graves of Early Settlers

In 1996, archaeologists also uncovered two graves. Preliminary analysis suggested that they were the burials of a European man and woman. The man, who was the victim of a massive gunshot wound to his lower leg, died between the age of 17 to 20. The woman died in her mid- to late- thirties. Both were buried in coffins, and the early and sparse nature of the artifacts, particularly from the male's burial shaft, suggested that they might have died during the early years of the settlement.

Ballistic tests indicated that the scatter of lead shot found in the man's leg wound could not be from an accidental, self-inflicted gunshot wound, and he was, therefore, deliberately killed or a victim of friendly fire. Recent scientific analysis of a sample of his bone produces conflicting evi-

Figure 2. Aerial photograph of James Fort excavation, fall 2000.

dence concerning his country of origin, and consequently, his date of death. Carbon isotope testing suggested that he was either native-born or from some country other than England. Therefore, he could not have been among the number of men who died in the summer of 1607.[4] However, another test for lead, strontium and oxygen isotopes suggested that he grew up in the United Kingdom, probably in the southwest of England or Wales.[5] The hexagonal shape of his coffin, a type believed by some to date no earlier than 1650, also suggests that he died much later than 1607.[6] On the other hand, a recent carbon reading places his date of death very early in the 17th century.

The woman immediately adjacent to the man was buried in an a-line, gable-lidded coffin, a type common to the early 17th century. Her carbon isotopic bone tests indicated she was an immigrant and her carbon date of death more toward the mid-17th century.[7]

Cellar Building and Associated Artifacts

During the past three seasons, excavations focused on an L-shaped pit located at the end of a 50-ft. palisade wall trench extending east of the east wall of the triangular Fort. The total excavation of that feature discovered that the pit was, in fact, a cellar built in two phases under a superstructure supported by fairly regularly spaced upright posts. More postholes show the outline of a room extending to the north of the cellar section and beyond that, a third room with a brick fireplace foundation in the southwestern corner. The brick hearth in the northernmost section shows evidence that it was rebuilt once.

Figure 3. Overhead view of the "trading post/workshop" in the Fort's southeastern extension.

Excavations in 2000 were able to trace the full extent of the building and revealed that a palisade ditch extends to the north from the northwest corner of the building. All of this showed plainly as soil stains in the clay, despite the fact that the area originally encompassed by the north end of the structure was part of the 17th- and 18th-century churchyard cemetery. A total of twenty-six grave shaft outlines were found. Many of the graves were dug through a clay floor layer in the building's northern two rooms. A curious brick platform or fireplace appeared along the east wall line of the north room, and 31 copper jettons were found within and around the northern rooms. Jettons are coin-like objects originally used for calculating on gridded boards. The great number and variety found at Jamestown suggests that they were reused as Indian trade items or perhaps as substitute currency.

A very rare, mint condition 1607 to 1609 silver James I halfpenny also was found associated with the building. Its condition indicates that it was probably dropped not long after it was minted, so it could well have been brought over by someone during the early supply voyages and used for a means of exchange.

In any case, the jettons and even the coin suggest that the building was in existence early and may have functioned as a trading post, a tavern, or some other public or commercial building. The hearths suggest some of the space might have been a common kitchen or workshop. However, there was no industrial waste in enough quantity on the floor to reveal what "work" may indeed have been carried out there. Of course cooking, baking, grain drying and perhaps brewing would leave no obvious waste. In the late 1620s Captain John Smith wrote: "some [settlers] malt the Indian corn, others Barley, of which they make strong Ale…"[8]

The nature and dates of artifacts in the cellar fill may connect the abandonment of the building or at least its cellar with the major cleanup ordered by Governor De la Warre in June of 1610, when he arrived with the men and supplies that saved the colony from abandonment.[9] It should be noted, however, that the date of the deposits could only be said to date *after* 1610, not necessarily *in* 1610.

Even with De La Warre's reported commitment to revitalizing the Fort, it is difficult to explain why *all* of the major subsurface footprints of the Fort buildings would be abandoned presumably during other construction. This is especially puzzling since the chronicler, William Strachey, in 1610 describes the Fort so precisely as still being triangular in form. Yet Strachey also wrote that the Fort was "lately brought to perfection" presumably by the efforts of De la Warre's men. Strachey held that the Fort was a triangular shape with two 300-ft. sides on the north and a 420-ft. side on the south made of "planks and strong posts".[10]

Perhaps the explanation lies in Strachey's earlier description of the town, written about what he saw on May 20, 1610, when he arrived with the previously shipwrecked party from Bermuda. He makes a strong point

Figure 4. 1607-1609 silver James I halfpenny.

that the town was in shambles with the main gate off the hinges, and the houses and palisade torn down and cut into firewood.[11]

It is significant that previous excavations indicated that the east wall of the Fort was purposely removed, possibly as a result of this desperate gathering of firewood.[12] Of course, the removal left the whole settlement wide open to attacks from the Powhatan warriors unless the east palisade had become an interior wall, rendered obsolete by the "five-sided" Fort built after the 1608 fire.[13]

In any case, if an exterior wall was down, then it is understandable, as Strachey remarked, that the Indians would kill anyone who ventured from their "blockhouse", the only protected place left to hide out.[14] The "blockhouse" could mean, of course, that the survivors were confined to the blockhouse that had been built near the isthmus at the extreme western end of the island or the blockhouse on Back River. But it also is possible that the settlers were seeking safety in the cellar building or buildings in the Fort which had become, in a sense, a blockhouse or Fort house when the palisades were gone.

Church Graveyard Boundaries

Archaeologists also uncovered grave shaft outlines all across the northern rooms of the building and surrounding it. Most of these were located north of a line of postholes that marked at least four of the several periods of graveyard fence construction. Major fence posts were spaced at nine-foot intervals, and there is some indication that fences from the four periods of construction maintained the same southern graveyard boundary

Figure 5. Excavation area within the bounds of the south palisade of James Fort.

line until an iron fence was installed for the observance of the 300th anniversary of Jamestown in 1907. This fence also followed the same southern line for some distance. Twenty-five graves were also found between the projection of the several fences and the river. The post line and graves also extended to the extreme eastern edge of the excavation, so the full extent of the burial ground in that direction remains unknown.

Southeast Bulwark Area

During the 2000 season, excavations also expanded into the interior of the Fort to the west of the southeast bulwark in an attempt to define other building locations that were, according to one account, extending in a line some 24 to 30-ft. from the palisade. Unfortunately, all that archaeologists could determine by digging in the area was that a number of ground disturbances likely wiped out any building traces. These included plowing, road grading since the 18th century, and the removal of clay three feet below the present grade from a pit that was probably dug in 1861 to accumulate dirt to form part of the nearby Civil War earthwork. The Civil War period clay quarry seems to have been filled back in, perhaps as part of the landscape improvements made in preparation for the installation of the John Smith statue and the reconstruction of the brick church prior to the 1907 Jamestown anniversary. At least three postholes of pre-pit date, a north-south ditch and six graves survived the various disturbances, but the digging of the pit obscured any relationship to remains from the James Fort period that may have existed there.

Figure 6. Excavation tracing the east palisade trench (arrow) of the Fort exposed the upper surface of what may be the north bulwark.

7

West Palisade Area

The excavation along the projected line of the Fort's west palisade north of the church tower provided better news. Previous testing in that area exposed a section of the palisade and a deposit of wood ash. The palisade section indicated that it had been dug out not too long after it was erected.[15]

The charcoal was dated to the period 1580 to 1620, suggesting that this burned material came from the fire that seriously damaged the Fort in 1608.[16] Recent excavation determined that the burned area was part of a large deposit of more charcoal and decayed organic material that may be at the terminus of the east palisade line of the Fort. Actually, the palisade in that area, which has been located but not yet excavated, seems to terminate at that point which is exactly 200 ft. from its southern end at the southeast bulwark.

This measurement may be extremely meaningful if the palisade was once connected to a structure perhaps now marked by the charcoal-laced black soil stain. Given the 200-ft. marker and the stain, it is possible that the north bulwark of the Fort or a watchtower stood there. Consequently, the 300-ft. measurement reported by William Strachey, in 1610, for the two landward sides of the triangular Fort was a total measurement that included two 50-ft. diameter bulwarks. (The southeast bulwark, found archaeologically, defines a 50-ft. circle.)

If that is the case, then the triangular Fort is much smaller than previous estimates. Actually, it is closer to the half acre in size that Strachey estimated, despite the fact that he said his measurements only referred to the curtain. Technically, the term "curtain" means the distance of the wall between bulwarks.

It should be pointed out that the black stain appears to be later in time than two ditches that it appears to cut through, which casts some doubt on it having anything to do with a bulwark standing there in 1608. However, artifacts found on the surface of the feature all date to the early Fort period.

Statehouse Building Study

Excavations in the 2000 season also began to systematically explore an unmarked burial ground located on the extreme western end of the APVA property beneath the foundations of the traditional site of the late 17th-century statehouse. Enough records of the statehouse building exist to provide some of its chronology and therefore, the date of the last burials. In 1694, a patent granted the land and ruins of three houses located between the "statehouse" and the "country house" to Philip Ludwell.[17] There is no question as to the location of this patent, which is a 1.5 acre lot that lies today among the central part of the massive three-part foundation, just west of the APVA Rediscovery Center (Yeardley House). The eastern end of this complex served as the "statehouse," and it is likely that the "country house" on the west served some governmental function as well.

The name "country house" meant that it belonged to the "country" or did at one time, or at least technically was owned by the Colony.

In 1698, the statehouse at Jamestown burned, and the the capital moved to Williamsburg the following year. It is likely that the statehouse that burned stood on the APVA foundation. There is no direct record, however, of where the government meeting building or buildings were at the time of the fire. It appears that buildings were not rebuilt on the foundations of the APVA statehouse foundations, even though the James City County Court still functioned at Jamestown until 1715. There is a reference to the removal of bricks from the statehouse ruins at Jamestown to be used for construction in Williamsburg. There also is evidence that some public governmental meetings were held in the APVA statehouse complex in the mid-1650s, indicating perhaps that the building existed by that date and perhaps as early as 1645.[18] In any case, while the assembly, council and court were held at various other Jamestown buildings at various times, it is clear that the APVA Ludwell-Statehouse complex served a public governmental function.

The next reference of importance to the complex followed an excavation of the foundations by Col. Samuel Yonge in 1903, recorded in his book, *The Site of Old Jamestown*, published in 1907.[19] In it, he describes what he found and includes a photo of one of the cellars and a drawing of the foundation he uncovered. It is important to note that based on what he found, he concluded that the building burned, it was built in three stages from west to east, and the eastern section could well match the description of the governmental functions of various spaces recorded in a document signed by "T.M." in 1694.[20] While the excavation was crude by modern standards, this work and his study of erosion and other patents at Jamestown were remarkably thorough and insightful. In any event, the foundations were capped with reinforced concrete, enclosed with a wrought iron fence still in place today, and left exposed above ground for interpretation.

In the early 1950's, the APVA and the National Park Service seriously considered reconstruction of the statehouse section of the foundation complex for the 350th celebration of Jamestown's founding. This plan led to two NPS archaeological investigations of the eastern foundation. Archaeologist Louis Caywood led the first excavation in 1954. He basically dug along the exposed eastern end of the foundation opening trenches three feet on either side of the brickwork. He found evidence of a partition wall, undetected by Yonge, burned floor joists, some roofing tiles and slate. He also recovered bones from six graves.

NPS archaeologist, Joel Shiner, took over the excavations the following year to explore the cemetery component of the site. He cleared away all of the topsoil and whatever accumulated building debris Caywood had missed down to the top of pre-building subsoil in order to locate and test these additional graves. Shiner found 70 grave outlines and uncovered the bones from seven.

Figure 7. 2000 Excavation of the Ludwell Statehouse foundation.

Both Caywood and Shiner concluded that the graves predated the building of the statehouse group probably by enough years to have erased all memory of the unmarked burial ground. Shiner concluded that the sometimes helter-skelter orientation of many of the graves might indicate that they were from the 1609 to 1610 winter of the "Starving Time." The remains from these excavations were re-examined indicating that of

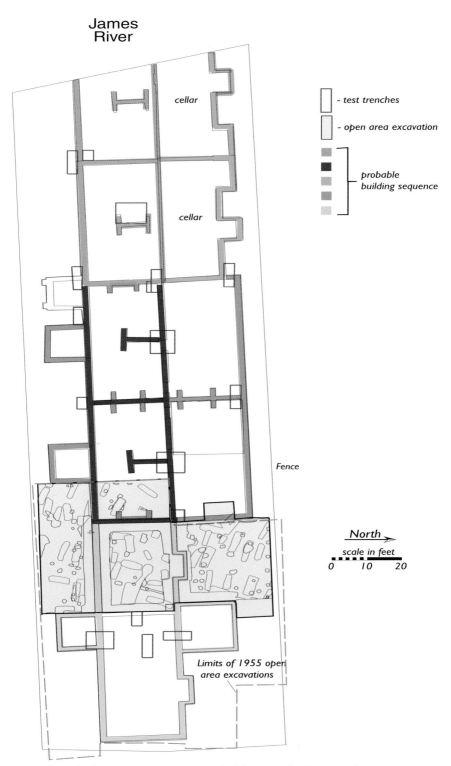

James
River

cellar

cellar

- test trenches

- open area excavation

probable
building sequence

Fence

North

scale in feet

0   10   20

Limits of 1955 open
area excavations

Figure 8. Construction sequence of the Ludwell Statehouse foundation complex.

11

Figure 9. Testing at key points along the Ludwell State-house foundations in 2000 determined sequence of construction where different periods of brick foundations walls came together.

the six skeletons that could be reliably studied, there were three males and three females, the women ranging in age from 15 to 34 and the men 15 to 19 years old at death.[21]

APVA excavations began in the summer of 2000 to study both the statehouse foundations and the earlier unmarked burial ground. A number of test trenches at strategic locations along the foundations uncovered by Yonge in 1903 proved his building construction sequence to be valid; the building was built over time from west to east with additions to the south. This was clear from inspecting wall junctions revealing which wall was an addition to a wall already standing.

Excavations within the foundations of H-shaped chimneys inside the central foundation also revealed evidence of a fire that destroyed at least the interior of the structure, despite the extensive digging by Yonge, the capping of the foundations, and probably earlier 19th century plowing. This testing also recovered roofing materials, suggesting that the easternmost building roof was covered with an inner-locking type of ceramic roof shingle known as pan tile, while the buildings to the west had either flat tiles or flat slate shingles.

APVA Statehouse Burial Study

The APVA's decision to study the unmarked burial ground lying beneath the statehouse foundations was predicated on the assumption that systematic recovery and preservation of a statistically valid sample of individual burials would make it possible to construct an early Jamestown population profile, of which there is little or no other record. This would include details on the ratio of females to males, ancestry, social and economic status, life expectancy, foreign to native birth ratios, general health, disease, causes of death, burial customs and possibly dates of death. This data also could be compared to other broader studies of 17th-century burials in the Chesapeake region and provide researchers with the earliest evidence of the Euro-American population in order to measure change over time and across the region.

About 50 percent of the sample was recovered initially, and the results almost immediately confirmed that many of these burials were made during times of stress. Some potentially were from the Starving Time winter of 1609 to 1610 at Jamestown where only 60 of 215 survived.[22]

Coffins were used for a few burials, but most individuals were buried in only a shroud. This was a common practice in late 16th-and early 17th-century England as coffins were expensive and typically purchased only by wealthy families for funerals. While there were many deep graves containing carefully positioned individuals, a number of graves were rather shallow and some individuals appear to have been placed in the shaft in a careless manner. This may have been due to a desire to minimize contact with the bodies of the deceased.

Figure 10. Testing of chimney foundations in the Statehouse complex revealed undisturbed burned layers of building debris possibly from the burning of Jamestown during Bacon's Rebellion in 1676.

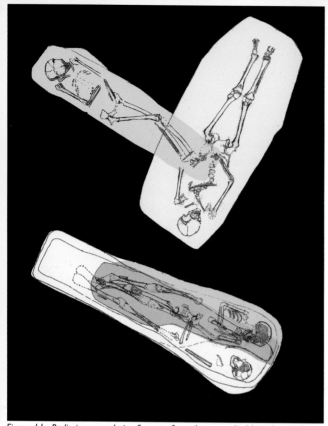

Figure 11. Preliminary analysis of graves from the unmarked burial ground beneath the Ludwell Statehouse foundation complex suggests that many of them were dug during times of rapid death. A number of the graves held two skeletons (left) and some were carelessly laid in hastily dug shallow grave shafts.

Two burials provide evidence for the presence of clothing, which indicates that these individuals were not undressed, washed and wrapped in a shroud as was customary for the time. This is strong evidence that while the living colonists felt bound to provide a "proper burial," in some instances they did it as quickly and with as little direct contact as possible. A number of grave shafts appear to have been purposefully reused for second burials, and several burials actually cut through earlier burials, suggesting that there was a significant time difference between the early and later burials and/or that no grave markers were used to identify individual graves.

Initial analysis indicates that most of the skeletons are males with only a few females present. The age at death varies considerably. Most appear to be adult males, but the sample also includes infants, adolescents, young adults and middle-aged adults. There is some evidence for childhood malnutrition and disease, and the development of muscle attachment sites on many of the skeletons indicates that they were regularly engaging in strenuous, physical activity. Initial impressions, therefore, suggest a mostly male, working class population.

Future scientific analysis, which will include chemical and DNA testing, promises to more precisely address these early conclusions and produce a more complete population profile.

CHAPTER 2   by J. Eric Deetz

"...set upon cratchets..."

By the summer of 2000, APVA Jamestown Rediscovery archaeologists had investigated the remains of two complete buildings (Structures 160 and 165) that confidently date to the early James Fort period (see figure 1 above).[23] Both structures were built using earthfast construction techniques, where the main structural posts of various sizes were placed directly into the ground without footings. Today, all that remains of the buildings are the soil stains left by the rotted timbers. In many ways, these two buildings are quite different from most other structural remains found elsewhere in the Chesapeake Bay region from later periods.[24] To date, the archaeological remains of over 250 earthfast structures have been excavated in the Chesapeake region. These architectural footprints vary in ways that suggest differing construction techniques and floor plans, and they offer comparative data with which to assess the earlier Jamestown building remains.

Structure 160

Structure 160 is defined by 26 postholes forming a rectangular pattern measuring 55 ft. by 18 ft. with a floor plan that likely included two rooms, a hall and a parlor. The main posts were not placed exactly opposite of each other, which indicates the posts were individually set. In later Chesapeake buildings, the posts are directly opposite each other, suggesting that they were raised together with a ceiling tie-beam connecting them. This apparently is not a type of construction used at Jamestown. Also the holes at Jamestown were not uniformly deep, another requirement of later tie beam construction. Another peculiar aspect of the Jamestown Strucure 160 is that the posts along each wall deviate significantly from a straight line. This random alignment makes it difficult to separate the interior space into whatever room plan existed. However, there is good evidence of at least two rooms. Extra interior posts in the smaller of the two rooms suggest that a crude wooden chimney frame stood there.

Architectural historian F.W.B. Charles describes post patterns found at English medieval house sites as similar to Strucutre 160.[25] He speculates that the post pattern suggests a type of construction where the carpenters built the roof, then hoisted it into position on natural forked timbers or "cratchets." Thus, the perimeter of the roofline determines the post placement. Any irregularities in timbers used for the wall/roof plate would dictate similar irregular alignment of the wall posts. Also the Jamestown posts were as slight as three inches in diameter which seems

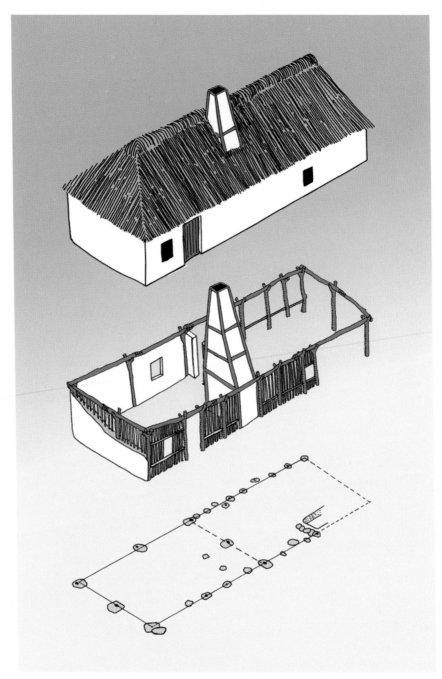

Figure 12. Conjectural drawing of Structure 160 as a mud and stud building.

to suggest that the building would be too weak to support the roof. This was probably not a problem since heavy clay walls on an inner sapling frame (wattle and daub) could conceivably bear considerable weight.

The varying depths and alignment of the posts, no tie-beam pairs, and no regular bays in Structure 160 all seem to be typical features of cratchet construction. Other evidence of cratchets is the placement of repair posts. Additional soil stains within the postholes indicated the posts in Structure 160 were repaired using the same hole as the original. Because the posts on a cratchet building are not fastened to the rest of the frame (the fork is the sole "joint), they are easily removed. More complex joinery would require repair to be adjacent to the original posts and would have left a double posthole footprint.

According to John Smith, the Jamestown cratchet construction is exactly the type of building that was erected at the Fort in the earliest period. In remembering the 1608 church, he described it as "a homely thing like a barn, set upon cratchets covered with rafts, sedge, and earth; so also was the walls." He continues with a description of the houses: "the best of our houses of the like curiosity but the most part much worse workmanship."[26] In this description Smith gives the impression that the structures in the early days were marginal at best. Yet, while the archaeological footprint of Structure 160 indicates a fairly informal structure, it still conforms to a broader medieval vernacular time-proven tradition.

Structure 165

The posthole pattern for Structure 165 delineates a building that was 17 ft. by 70 ft. It is comprised of 18 postholes defining three cells: a 24-ft. long northern cell, a 17-ft. long center cell and a 29-ft. long southern cell. There is a cellar under the southernmost cell and a brick hearth between the center and northern cells. As in Structure 160, the postmolds indicate slight framing. No post measured more than 6 in. in diameter and they were all round. Unlike Structure 160, there is no conclusive evidence pointing to the way in which these posts were erected. The slightly more formal post alignment allows for the possibility of tie-beam pairs, yet the random bottom elevations of the posts support the argument that the posts were set individually.

A set of stairs cut into subsoil in the northwest corner provided access to the cellar. Since the cellar was under the southern third of the structure it would have had a ceiling. Consequently, the southern third of the structure had a wooden floor. The cellar itself shows signs of being constructed in two phases and was filled in all at once at some point early in Jamestown's history.[27] Sunk into the floor of the cellar were two half barrels presumably used as sumps

Figure 13. Spanish sailors erecting cratchet buildings after a shipwreck in the late 16th-century.

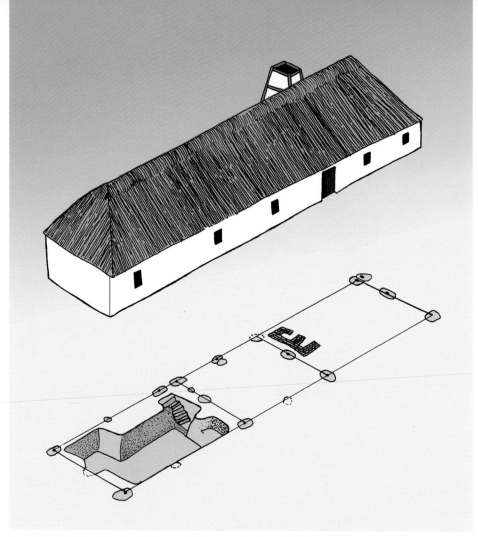

Figure 14. Conjectural drawing of Structure 165 as a mud and stud building.

to collect seeping water. The section of the building north of the hearth had a prepared floor consisting of roughly eight inches of a mixture of ash and clay. The artifacts found associated with this room and floor appear to be debris lost there during occupation. For the most part, these included small fragments of bone, small shards of ceramics, lead shot, and sprue, and 31 copper-alloy casting counters or jettons — an incredible amount. In addition, 54 jettons were found in the cellar fill, and 14 were found in other contexts relating to the structure, for a total of 99 jettons. Since jettons could have been used for trading with the Indians, they could be a clue to the building's function. Unlike Structure 160, which was inside the perimeter of the 1607 Fort, Structure 165 was built into the palisade and was part of the Fort perimeter. A section of palisade connects it to the east bulwark, and there are traces of palisade leading north from the northwest corner of the building. This is the section of Fort that may

Figure 15. Typical late-16th, early 17th-century jetton

very well be what Smith referred to when he said the Fort was "reduced to a five square form" late in 1608.[28] Being on the Fort perimeter, places the building on the fringe of security, where perhaps it functioned as a buffer where Indians and settlers could trade freely without risking the Fort's security. That being the case, the entrance to the structure was an important feature.

It is not clear from the posthole pattern alone where the main doorway for Structure 165 was located. However, the location of the doorway can be inferred from the location of the chimney in the northernmost room (see above Chap. 2 and *Jamestown Rediscovery VI*) and artifacts found in a location east of the chimney foundation. Together, these suggest that this building had what was known as a lobby entrance. This was a room plan common in 17th-century England and later in New England, where an exterior main entrance door opened into a small room, the lobby, which was closed off from the rest of the house by an inner door next to the chimney.[29] Hence, there would be some means of controlling access to the inner rooms of the building, and consequently, the interior of the Fort extension.

The discovery of a bottle containing just pebbles found buried here adds to the likelihood that this was the location of the entranceway. This may be a witch-bottle, not an uncommon find on post-Medieval house sites in England.[30] Usually, witch-bottles were stoneware jugs filled with sharp items such as nails or pins, and they often contained the urine of the person believed to be under the spell of a witch or who was to be protected from a witch. They typically date to the 17th century with the earliest examples dating to the late 16th century. Usually, they were buried under the hearth or threshold, as both were considered possible points of entry for witches. Witches were a very real concern in the belief systems of 17th-century English. New England Puritan luminaries Cotton and Increase Mather both wrote extensively on the subject of witchcraft and specifi-

Figure 16. The existence of witches was a reality in the 17th-century.

19

cally mentioned witches' bottles as counter magical devices. No analysis has been done yet on the soil or stones from the interior of the bottle, but if it was intended as counter magic, it could well indicate the placement of a doorway.[31]

Both structure 160 and structure 165 fit the description of the early houses offered by William Strachey, Secretary of the Colony from 1610-1611. In his *True Reportory* published in 1612, he wrote:

> "*Our people do dress their chambers and inward rooms, which make their houses so much the more handsome. The houses have wide and large country chimneys.*"

Later in the same text he adds:

> "*Whilst they were, as at first, pargeted and plastered with bitumen or tough clay*"[32]

Houses were more than one room ("chambers and inward rooms") with stick and mud smoke hoods ("country chimneys") such as the type commonly used in rural buildings in England at the time of Jamestown's establishment.[33] In *Cotgraves Hard Word Dictionary* of 1611, pargeted is defined as whitewashed, and bitumen is defined as a fast and clammy earth, clay or loam.[34] Strachey's description suggests a multiple room house covered with clay and then whitewashed. Visually, this type of structure would be a departure from the image usually put forth of the Jamestown houses. They would have born a greater resemblance to Devon cottages than the half-timbered, clapboard cabins of the 1950's Sidney King paintings. These structures also share a long narrow floor plan similar to long narrow buildings constructed at Baffin Island by the Frobisher expedition 1576-1578,[35] Maine's Popham Colony in 1607,[36] and the Phipps site from the 1630's, also in Maine.[37] In a frontier situation, economical, long barracks style buildings, suitable for multiple uses, make sense.

Influences that led to creation of the classic earthfast houses of archaeological 17th-century Virginia have been sought in architectural traditions as far flung as German Grubenhausen, Native and Afro Caribbean structures, as well as the vernacular traditions of the British Isles. The James Fort structural evidence now provides a key to understanding the precursor of this tradition. It best matches a building style common in the post-medieval East Midlands region of England, mostly the eastern half of the county of Lincolnshire.[38]

The construction of a mud and stud building starts with a framework of slight timbers. Between the uprights there were cross pieces to which were fastened vertical slats that would hold the clay walls that would eventually help bear the load of the roof. Unlike other traditional wattle and daub or half-timbered buildings, the clay is continued out beyond the posts to create a smooth uninterrupted clay exterior. This exterior surface is then whitewashed with a mixture of lime and animal fat for a waterproof surface that would need to be recoated every year or so. The roofs are traditionally a light framework of natural pole rafters put together to form a hip or half-hipped roof, which is then thatched.

Because the exterior of these structures hid the internal framework, mud and stud buildings were not always recognized for what they were. This misidentification has been compounded by the common practice of encasing these buildings in brick, which was done from the Victorian period until the recent past. The true earthfast nature of these structures was also somewhat hidden. As the original posts rotted over time, it was necessary to place brick underpinning along the base of the walls of many of them. This hid the original construction techniques from the casual observer.

The true nature of the mud and stud building tradition has come to light as a result of preservation laws in the United Kingdom that required the study of all older buildings. Architect Rodney Cousins has determined that out of the over 300 examples dating from the late-16th to the 18th centuries that are still standing in Lincolnshire, at least half are of earthfast construction.[39]

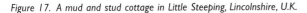
Figure 17. A mud and stud cottage in Little Steeping, Lincolnshire, U.K.

This strong Lincolnshire regional tradition becomes even more important since many of the early American settlers came from here. John Smith came from Alford in the middle of the East Midland region. It is likely that William Laxon, one of the carpenters on the first voyage, was from Lincolnshire,[40] and Richard Dixon, John Dodds, and Nathaniel Peacock, all first settlers at Jamestown, were also from the region.[41] Many of the settlers of New England also hailed from Lincolnshire. Many of the Separatists that settled Plymouth colony were not only from the area around the city of Boston in Lincolnshire, but many were jailed there for their religious beliefs before they left for Holland and later the New World. Many of the puritans that came to Massachusetts Bay colony with John Winthrop originated in region as well.[42] It should come as no surprise that a region that contributed so many of its native sons and daughters to the settlement of America should also have contributed a strong local building tradition that would lend itself well to the needs of arriving colonists.[43]

At the close of the 16th century, England was in the middle of what architectural historian W.M. Barley has called a housing revolution.[44] The nouveau riche of the Elizabethan era were busying themselves building extravagant halls, and the yeoman farmers and wage laborers were benefiting from a general upscale trend in housing styles. At this time, the landscape was still dotted with smaller buildings from medieval times. It was during this era of change that the future settlers of Jamestown were born and came of age. Though most of them came from the more rural surroundings of southeastern England, they would have been equally familiar with the most elaborate buildings of their region such as the Gosnold family's Otley Hall or the traditional Hall and Parlor farmhouses of the East Midlands in Lincolnshire. Along with the saws, chisels, and axes needed to construct a town upon their arrival, on May 13, 1607, laborers and gentleman alike brought to Jamestown a tool every bit as important, a mental template of what towns and houses should look like.

The question remains, "What did they look like?" For the answer we need to look to the documentary evidence, as well as the archaeological remains. The structural remains at James Fort are among the evidence of the earliest English buildings found in North America. This makes them a true representation of the vernacular tradition from which they were derived.

Finding out how the settlers adapted their building traditions in the face of the realities of the new Virginia environment and how their buildings were influenced by the Virginia Indian culture remains a major expectation for future Jamestown Rediscovery research.

Chapter 3 by Seth W. Mallios

EVERY ARTIFACT COUNTS

When told that excavations at the site of 1607 James Fort have produced well over 350,000 artifacts, visitors usually ask, "Which one do you think is most important?" For good reason, each *Jamestown Rediscovery* staff member has a different answer—the James Fort collection is that rich, and the research process that democratic.

Without a doubt, individual objects tell revealing Jamestown stories. For example, a butchered horse bone from an early trash pit suggests that famished colonists ate whatever foods were at hand in order to survive the

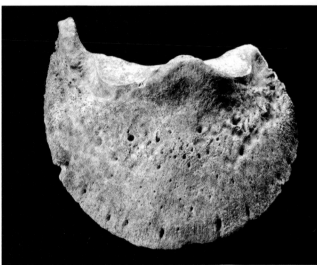

Figure 18. A horse hoof uncovered in a Fort-Period cellar

devastating "Starving Time" winter of 1609/1610. Likewise, a finely decorated silver tool known as an "ear picker" made in the shape of a dragon-like sea creature illustrates that its early 17th-century owner lived in an Atlantic world thought to be laced with fantastical monsters.

Although every object from the site offers insight into the past, the James Fort collection is far too enormous to understand by considering one object at a time. No matter how informative a single object is by itself, its significance often can be comprehended more completely against the background of the thousands of other objects found with it. In fact, a unique find can be recognized as unique only when the great number of things associated with it, indicate that it is exceptional.

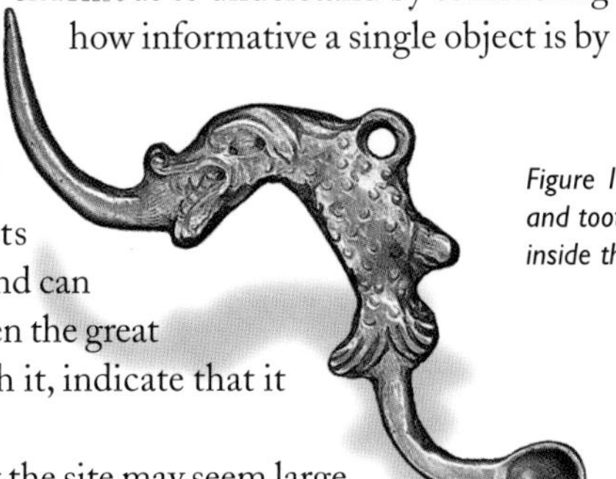

Figure 19. This ornate ear and tooth pick was found inside the Fort extension.

Similarly, an individual find at the site may seem large, heavy, or well-made, but it can be more clearly defined by comparison to other items that are smaller, lighter, or less well-made. In that sense, all artifacts, from the tiniest glass bead to the big-

Figure 20. Early colonists often trimmed sheets of copper into square pendants, like this one, and traded these items to native Powhatans for food.

gest cannon ball, are relative to each other. By taking a rigorous look at an entire collection, archaeologists can sort out what is truly exceptional from the ordinary.

No matter how small, fragmented, or seemingly insignificant, each artifact plays an important role in revealing the patterns of past life. Like the thousands of individual brush strokes that together form the images in an impressionistic painting, every single artifact helps create a picture of the past. By comparing the quantity of different kinds of objects, archaeologists can reveal facets of life that are not necessarily clear through considerations of only "one-of-a-kind" items.

Consider an individual scrap of sheet copper, one of over six thousand pieces found in sealed deposits at the James Fort site during the last seven years of excavation. To understand more fully what this fragment might reveal about 17th-century Jamestown, it is important to compare it to the total of the site's other copper scraps in terms of space, time, and form. This type of comparison will determine the relative quantities of copper scraps found across the site and how copper scraps might have changed in number, design, or chemical make-up through time.

Such patterns exist for copper and for some other types of artifacts found at Jamestown, even though later events altered the landscape of the site. Farmers routinely tilled the soil here in the years following abandonment of the English town. Their plows blended the top foot or so of dirt.

This process resulted in the mixing of older artifacts from deeper in the ground with newer items from shallower areas and erased the uppermost foot of intact colonial deposits. The layer became a disturbed context, meaning that the items in it were moved around since Jamestown settlers first dropped them there. But all was not lost. Even though the farmers' plows stirred together debris from different time periods, the plowing did not move the artifacts far from where they were originally deposited horizontally. Consequently, the resulting "plowzone" soil layer still holds reliable evidence of past colonial life.

By studying the greater or lesser number of specific kinds of plowzone objects, like nails or bricks, grouped by uniform measurable spaces (10-ft. squares), archaeologists can reveal, in the case of nails and bricks, what might be the only remaining evidence of buildings that vanished long ago. The house timbers might have rotted away and plowing might have erased the stains in the soil marking the edges of old postholes, but the pattern of building debris could still pinpoint a structure's location and dimensions. Looking at other kinds of objects, the patterns could indicate how colonists used certain items and disposed of these materials.

For example, items deposited at the site predominantly during the Fort Period, 1607 to 1623, consisted of a wide assortment of bone, ceramics, metal, glass, and stone. A study of the relative quantities of certain types of objects proved to be particularly informative. The pottery under study included an English earthenware known as Border ware, stoneware crucibles, delftware jars designed for storing ointments and drugs, German stoneware jugs from Frechen, French flasks from Martincamp, and Spanish olive jars. The metal objects were cannon balls, copper scraps, fish hooks, jettons, lead cloth seals, lead shot and sprue, and musket rests. The chipped stone consisted of flint, and arrow and spear projectile points made of a variety of rock types.

Contour maps based on the number of objects studied and where they were found in the plowzone revealed a few general patterns. The total num-

Figure 21. The image to the left shows the profile of features that still have their original living surface. The one to the right offers a side view of the same features after they have been truncated by plowing.

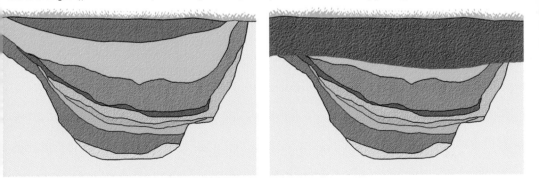

25

Figure 22. A sample of Fort-Period artifacts, including delftware apothecary jar, Martincamp neck fragment, crucible, Border ware candle stick, Bartmann jug fragment, copper scrap, cloth seal, lead shot, copper-alloy jetton, and fishhook.

ber of selected artifact types found in each 10-ft. square determined the placement of the contour lines. Overall, the patterns were identified by how well the contour lines respected the edges of the different Fort-Period features. Lines that ran in the same direction as the edges of a feature on the map indicated that the feature probably dated to the Fort Period. The feature, such as a Fort-Period palisade wall, would have acted as a barrier that confined an artifact-producing activity to either the inside or outside of the Fort wall. On the other hand, contour lines that went through a feature demonstrated that the feature was not prominent during the Fort Period. For example, a wall outline that was criss-crossed by numerous contour lines on the map revealed that the wall did not likely exist in the early 17th century.

The resulting contour map indicated a number of things:

1) The location of the objects conformed to the edges of three Fort-related elements:

       i) Structure 160, an earthfast building just inside of the Fort wall

       ii) Pit 3, possibly a powder magazine in the south bastion, and

       iii) The Fort's southeastern corner.

2) The distribution of the artifacts partially followed the border of the Fort's southern wall and eastern extension.

3) The pattern of items did not respect the triangular Fort's original eastern wall.

The pattern of early objects in the plowzone also provided additional evidence that Structure 160 was much longer than initially thought. Initially defined as a slightly trapezoidal 18.8-ft. by 25.5-ft. building supported by 10 posts that sunk into the ground, the structure's irregular shape hinted at alternative interpretations regarding its form.

Structure 160 was identified in 1995 as a Fort-Period building for a variety of reasons.[45] It was aligned with the fort's southern wall and was less than 12 ft. from the riverside palisade. In addition, the remains of

Structure 160 contained no artifacts from later time periods. The map's contour lines respected the building's boundaries, substantiating its Fort-Period designation.

The plowzone above Structure 160 contained few early items inside the building's nearly rectangular plan. Furthermore, the structure had a 10 to 20-ft. wide ring of early plowzone objects surrounding it. The ring of Fort-Period debris around Structure 160 suggested that its early colonial inhabitants deposited the items outside the building in traditional 17th-century broadcast refuse fashion. Archaeologist James Deetz first noted this pattern when studying early colonization in New England. Deetz wrote that, "all waste materials were simply thrown out, and often at what to us would be an alarmingly short distance from the door."[46]

The swath of early debris was present on the south, west, and north sides of the structure's defined postholes. The central gap in Fort-Period plowzone objects continued 16 ft. eastward. This pattern suggested that at some time during the building's existence it extended further to the east.

The recent discovery and excavation of Structure 165, an additional long and narrow building along the Fort's eastern extension, was so similar in its layout that it supports reconsideration of Structure 160, as well. Additional postholes to the east of Structure 160 corresponded with the wide gap in the contour map.

Figure 23. Archaeological plan of the James Fort site with Fort-Period artifact contours. Darker shading reflects high artifact densities; lighter areas signify lower artifact densities.

27

Contour lines generated from the plowzone's early artifacts aligned much more with the Fort's eastern extension and southern wall than with the original eastern wall. They ran mostly parallel to the southern wall and eastern extension, yet were perfectly perpendicular to the original eastern wall. This pattern suggested that the southern wall and eastern extension served as more substantial Fort boundaries that were used longer than the original eastern wall. Past excavations of the original eastern wall revealed that it had been dismantled.

To the contrary, excavations of parts of the southern wall and eastern extension indicated that these Fort posts had never been extracted.[47] Colonists probably dug or yanked out the posts of the original eastern wall. On the other hand, most of the timbers of the southern wall and eastern extension likely rotted in place. Also the location of early objects in the plowzone and the results of past excavations implied that the original eastern wall was very short-lived.

Figure 24. Two interpretations regarding the length of Structure 160. The plowzone analysis supports the image on the bottom.

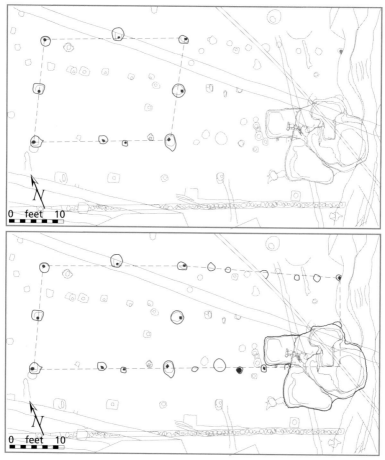

Figure 25. Sydney King's conjectural portrait of the extended English Fort at Jamestown Island shows the original eastern wall and extension standing at the same time. The plowzone study suggests, to the contrary, that once the extension was built the original eastern wall no longer acted as a significant barrier and was likely dismantled.

Historical eyewitness accounts describe James Fort at first as a three-sided palisade in 1607. Primary documents also reveal that by 1608 to 1609 the colonists had transformed the triangular Fort into a five-sided fortification/town.[48] These accounts led past scholars to believe that the original triangular James Fort had been enlarged with a rectangular addition to the east. Hypothetical reconstructions often included the original eastern wall as still standing within the expanded five-sided Fort. This does not seem to be the case.

The original eastern wall did not serve as a meaningful barrier inside of the five-sided Fort. More than likely, it was dismantled or destroyed at about the same time the Fort was transformed. The fire of early January 1608 that Captain John Smith described as burning "our Fort… and the most of our apparell, lodging and private provision" might have caused the need to rebuild and alter the overall shape of James Fort and its buildings.[49] Nevertheless, a primary historical account from 1610 offered triangular dimensions for the English fortifications at Jamestown Island.[50]

Erosion, earthmoving during the Civil War, and the construction of modern elements, like the sizable base to the John Smith monument, created variations in plowzone across the site. This complicated the study and made it necessary to determine the density of the number of Fort-Period objects per unit of plowzone volume. This additional step enabled accurate results even in areas with different amounts of plowzone. Regardless of past soil-moving disturbances, the traces of past everyday life were accessible through careful analysis of plowzone artifacts such as copper.

Copper played a significant role in relations between Jamestown colonists and the indigenous Powhatan population during the first half of the 17th century. Smith frequently described how the Powhatans cherished these metal objects. He also celebrated the success with which the English traded their copper items for native goods. Smith reported that, "for a copper kettle… [the Powhatans] will sell you a whole Countrey."[51]

Copper was a prestigious spiritual good for the Chesapeake natives. They believed that individuals who were buried with copper possessed a bountiful afterlife. Smith noted that low-status natives who were unable to obtain copper were thought "to not live after death, but rot in their graves like dead dogs."[52] The Powhatans so prized copper that they took the cadavers of their deceased chiefs and "their inwards they stuffe[d] with copper beads."[53] Smith also detailed how the Powhatans buried "their Kings… betwixt two mattes within their houses, with all… [their] copper."[54]

The English learned of native desires for copper when attempting to settle Roanoke Island in the 1580s. One of the local Roanoac chiefs, presumably speaking figuratively, told Captain Arthur Barlowe in 1584, that the small copper pendant he wore as a necklace "would defende him against his enemies' arrows."[55] Since the native leader paid his warriors in copper, the pendant was an extremely effective insurance policy.[56] Although three different English colonies failed in their attempts at permanently settling the Carolinas in the late 1500s, lessons learned from these endeavors regarding the importance of copper in native society were essential to Jamestown's success.

Figure 26. A sample of the thousands of copper items—including scraps, coins, jettons, and tubular beads—found in Fort-Period contexts.

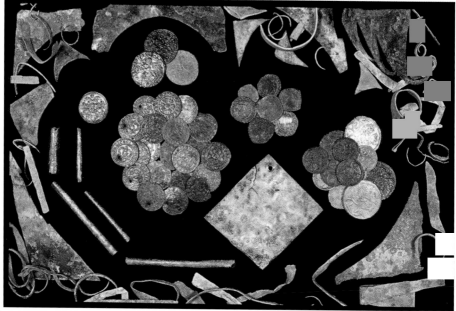

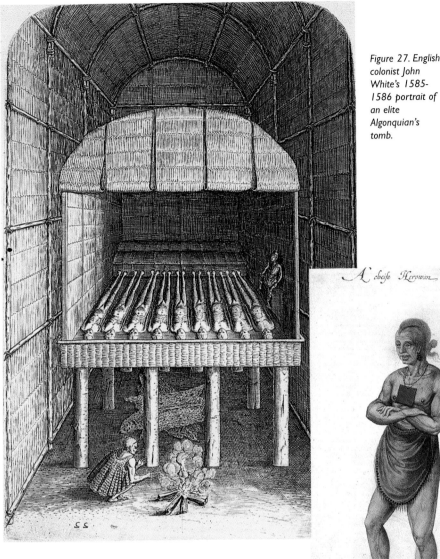

Copper scraps, the trimmings from the English manufacture of trade goods at Jamestown, are one of the most commonly found items at the site. The relationship between copper items and time is very strong. The more copper objects found in a given deposit, the earlier it was filled. This pattern includes all copper items, suggesting that other forms of the metal, such as jettons and pins, were used in early English/Powhatan exchange as well.

Figure 28. This elite Roanaoc native wore a copper pendant nearly identical to many uncovered at Jamestown. The portrait by John White might depict Granganimeo.

Mathematical measures indicate that over four-fifths of the variation in the amount of copper in a feature at the James Fort site is due to the time it was filled. The link between copper and time is so strong that the

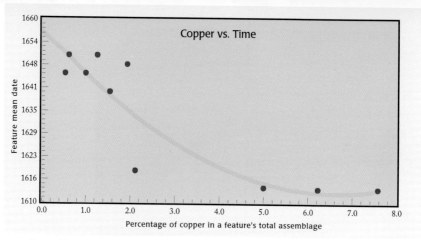

Figure 29. Scatter plot of copper and time. The points cluster closely about the equation line.

date of a deposit can be reliably estimated on the basis of how much copper is in it. The exact copper/time relationship at the site fits a mathematical curve that equates the percentage of copper in a feature with the date it was filled. The equation is: $y = 1.023x^2 - 13.625x + 1657.831$.[57]

To use the equation, first determine the percentage of copper in a feature by dividing the total number of objects in the feature by the number of copper items. Second, plug in this percentage as (x).[58] The resultant answer, (y), is the middle year that the feature was filled. For example, if a feature has no copper $(x = 0)$, its projected fill date is 1657. Since a feature cannot have a negative amount of copper, the latest context on which this dating technique can and should be used is 1657.

Figure 30. Map of Jamestown's hinterland.

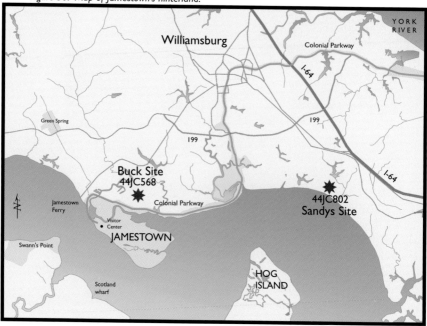

The equation, created on the basis of what was found in the vicinity of 1607 James Fort, was tested on two archaeological sites located off of Jamestown Island.[59] The Reverend Richard Buck Site (44JC568) was less than a mile north of Jamestown in an area known during the 17th century as "Neck of Land." Historical documents narrowed the probable occupation from 1624 to 1654. Distinct groups of colonists dug and used different wells at the site during its 20-year occupation. Application of the Jamestown copper equation to the artifact collection accurately estimated when the site was inhabited. It also placed the three wells in correct chronological order.[60] A similar application of the copper-dating technique to the artifacts from the George Sandys Site (44JC802) in Kingsmill Neck was equally promising. This site was most likely occupied from 1628 to 1638.[61] The copper equation projected the middle of the site occupation to be 1636, which is well within the historically documented occupation range. With such encouraging results, this dating tool will be used on other nearby sites from the first 60 years of the 17th century.

The way copper objects dwindled in number over time at sites in and around Jamestown during the 1600s, reflected in the sharp decline of the copper curve, offers insight into overall changes in the English/Powhatan copper trade. Early exchanges at James Fort were successful for both parties; each side felt it was getting a fair shake. Later trades, however, were undermined by certain European trade practices.

Smith complained in his writings about how some of his fellow colonists, especially visiting merchant sailors, repeatedly flooded the natives with copper items.[62] Glutting Powhatan society with copper objects devalued the metal and upset the native social order.[63] Copper no longer distinguished chiefs from their followers. In fact, this disruption in the balance of the copper trade contributed to the overall deterioration of English/Powhatan relations.

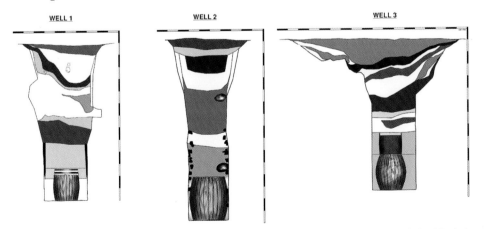

Figure 31. Profile maps of three wells found in close proximity to one another at the Reverend Richard Buck site.

Studies of the distribution patterns of certain groups of objects, such as copper, reveal the habits of *all* that lived within a given area, not just the *few* who could write. They also illustrate that no single item is necessarily more important than any other. Archaeology is a most democratic discipline. Americans may debate these days whether every vote counts in an election, but in archaeology there is no doubt that every artifact counts. In fact, it is only in the definition of normal everyday life that exceptional items, events, and people have any relevance whatsoever. Essentially, it is the ordinary that makes the extraordinary… extraordinary.

Research that emphasizes unique items and studies that rigorously examine the entire collection complement one another. Both approaches offer important insights into the enormous pool of artifacts from the site of 1607 James Fort. The proverb, "All that glitters is not gold," has an important double message for past and present Jamestown.[64] First, it reflects the colonists' obsession with discovering precious metals in Virginia. Smith noted in 1608 that:

"there was no talke, no hope, no worke, but dig gold, wash gold, refine gold, loade gold, such a bruit [rumor] of gold, that one mad fellow desired to be buried in the sands least they should by there art make gold of his bones."[65]

Secondly, it sums up the archaeological philosophy that unspectacular items, especially when grouped together, often yield valuable insights. Ironically, objects that shine the least—the many bits of pottery, metal, etc.—can be most informative. In terms of the insights they reveal about the past, they are, "Not gold, but golden things."… The answer to another commonly asked question at the site: "Have you found any gold yet?"

CHAPTER 4 by Beverly A. Straube

"But their victualls are their chiefest riches ..."

Previous *Jamestown Rediscovery* reports have discussed artifacts from the site that reflect trade between the colonists and the indigenous population. These have focused on the copper ornaments and glass beads that the colonists contributed to the intercultural exchange, but what about evidence of the goods they received in return?[66] A recent study of selected artifacts indicates that some of the materials excavated from the colonial contexts may have found their way into the Fort as gifts, trade items, or personal possessions of the Virginia Indians.

Figure 32. The colonists depended on an exchange of goods with the Indians to establish bonds of friendship and a steady supply of food.

Food

The historical records tell us that food was the foremost object of trade for the settlers during the first few years of settlement. In John Smith's opinion, of all the commodities the colonists received from the Indians, "their victuals are their chiefest riches."[67] There was no gold, no silver, and no secret passage to the Orient. But the Indians had "foule, fish, flesh, and their Country Corne", which, as it turned out, proved even more valuable to the starving and ill-supplied colonists. This was not entirely what the governing council of the Virginia Company, the corporation that was managing the colony, had envisioned, although it was part of the plan to have the native population provision Jamestown. The company's men were in Virginia primarily to make money for the investors. They were not to waste time laboring in agriculture when, for a few cheap trinkets, sustenance could be obtained from the Indians.[68] On one trading expedition, for instance, John Smith successfully traded 25 pounds of copper and 50 pounds of iron and beads for enough "bread, corne, flesh, fish and fowle" to feed 40 men for six weeks.[69]

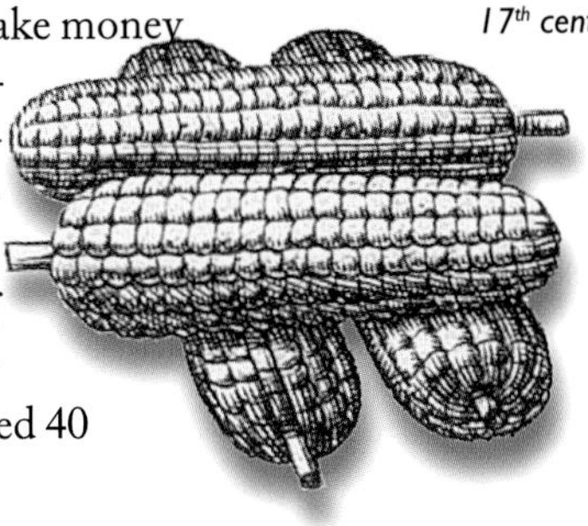

Figure 33. Corn was important to the survival of everyone living in Virginia in the early 17th century.

Figure 34. In the Native American society, the women were responsible for the cultivation of corn and its processing into food.

The most common foodstuff the early colonists mentioned obtaining from the native people was corn.[70] Corn was basic to the Indian diet because, with a relatively small investment in labor, abundant crops of high nutritional value could be produced that provided year-round nourishment. One historian has estimated that corn provided about 75 percent of the calories consumed by the Indians living in the Coastal Plain.[71]

Indian women, with the help of the elderly men and children, were responsible for the cultivation and processing of corn, although the men helped with the initial clearing of land. This task, according to John Smith, was the most difficult because "the Country naturally is overgrowne with wood."[72] The Indians planted corn from April through the middle of June, providing a sequence of harvests that lasted from August through October. Every ear of their corn was described by the colonists has having "betwixt 200 and 500 graines," each of which were in the form "of a man's tooth" though "somewhat thicker."[73]

The Powhatan favored boiled corn on the cob, which the English considered to be "green" or unripe. Throughout the winter months the Indians ate corn that had been dried by "roasting it in hot ashes." They would either boil this corn with beans "for a rare dish, they call *Pausarowmena,*" or they would make it into dried corn meal for use in cakes or soup. Colonist William Strachey related that even the "coare of the eare" or cob was consumed by being burned "to powder" and "mingling that in their meale." Strachey goes on to complain that the pulverized cob "never tasted well in bread, nor broth."[74] It is no wonder that this dish was not to the colonists' palate! The English were accustomed to eating their cereal grains in pottages[75] where the grain was either boiled in milk seasoned with sugar and spices or, for a thinner gruel, in water together with dried fruit. Buttered cereals were especially favored.[76]

In the first few years, the Jamestown settlement became very dependent upon corn for survival, often taking it by force from Indian groups who were reluctant to barter. Smith admits that most individuals reading about the great lengths the colonists went to "for a little corn" will think it strange. Without it, however, "the whole colony [would have] starved."[77] Unfortunately, organic material such as corn has little chance of surviving in the ground, so the archaeological record does not reflect the impor-

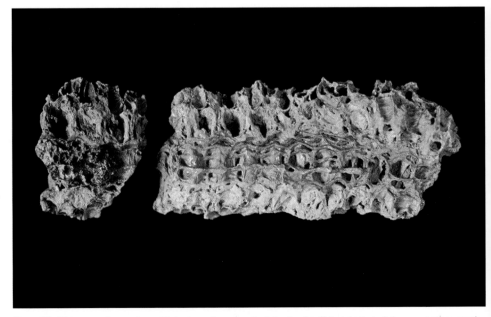

Figure 35. This corncob pseudomorph is the only remnant of the foodstuff that historical documentation reveals was so important to the early Jamestown colonists' survival.

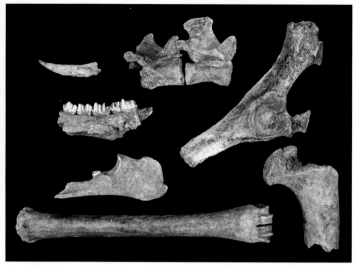

Figure 36. A sample of the ninety-one elements of deer bone that have been recovered from James Fort.

tance of this material to the early settlement. Only one fragment of an ear of corn has been excavated during the Jamestown Rediscovery excavations. It survived as a pseudomorph, or an "iron" corncob, created by the corrosion products of metal artifacts that had been buried with the corncob taking the form of the kernels as they decayed.

At times, the Indians also brought the colonists meat from the wide range of wild fauna that they hunted. John Smith writes that during one stretch of 16 days, "*the Countrie people brought us . . . 100 a day, of Squirrils, Turkyes, Deere, and other wilde beasts.*"[78]

An analysis of excavated animal bones, representing food that the colonists ate, has identified that "wildlife contributed half of the colonists' meat diet" within the first ten years of settlement.[79] The other half was comprised of domestic animals, such as pigs, cows, and chickens that were brought from England either as barreled stores of food or as breeding stock.

Some of the wild species eaten by the colonists was undoubtedly the result of trade with the Indians, but, without distinctive butchery marks that would signal native tools and/or techniques, there is no way to distinguish it from food the colonists acquired themselves. Certainly, many of the Englishmen in the Fort would have been adept at hunting; however, in Virginia, their weapons and their customary hunting methods were more successful with some prey than with others.

The colonists appear to have been the most proficient at hunting fowl; even surpassing the natives' ability to bag winged game. This advantage is illustrated in historical records when Powhatan requests that an Englishman re-

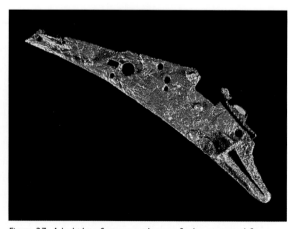

Figure 37. A lockplate from a snaphaunce fowler excavated from Structure 165. Its self-igniting ignition system gave it a distinct advantage over the matchlock gun.

Figure 38. The colonists appear to have relied on the Indians' expertise in hunting deer to provide them with most of their deer meat.

main at the Indian village Werowocomoco for the express purpose of shooting fowl for him.[80] Bird hunting was evidently difficult for the Indians since they would indiscriminately kill any fowl they were able to catch, including "fatt or leane, young or old in eggs, in breeding tyme, or however."[81]

The English success in birding can be attributed to the use of firearms. The type of gun commonly used for birding in England was the matchlock; but the snaphaunce fowler, which was first used in England in the early 17th century, was far more efficient. The snaphaunce was a self-igniting firearm that used the spark produced by flint striking steel to fire the gun. This provided a distinct advantage over the matchlock, which required an ever-burning fuse (matchcord) to fire it. The snaphaunce had a range of about 200 yards, "and it was easily turned into a military arm for the defence of or attack on fortified positions."[82] Even so, these early guns were heavy, unwieldy, and highly inaccurate by modern standards. To compensate for the inaccuracy, the common practice was to load a handful of small lead bullets known as shot, rather than a single ball. When the gun was fired, the shot would spread out in a circular spray, greatly increasing the likelihood that something would be hit. Jamestown colonist Strachey records that, with the use of small shot, the men were able to shoot five or six partridges out of a tree at one time.[83] In addition, Smith and two other men are recorded as having killed 148 fowl on one occasion with just three attempts each.[84]

If the colonists had the upper hand in birding, the opposite appears to be true in hunting the large game such as deer. The men were not accustomed to stalking deer in the wild, as they had to do in Virginia. Deer had become so scarce in England by the early 17th century that deer hunting had become an organized event that was reserved for the privileged few. It was "deemed necessary to breed and protect (deer) in parks established by royal licence, enclosed with pales, hedges, and ditches, and protected by gamekeepers."[85] Lower class individuals were involved in the hunt only peripherally as servants or tenants of the gentlemen, so, for the most part, only the Jamestown gentlemen would have been experienced deer hunters.

The common method for deer hunting in the English preserves was on horseback and using dogs to drive the game into nets. A variety of weapons were employed including javelins, swords, daggers, longbows, crossbows and guns. Many, such as King James, considered the use of firearms in hunting deer to be distasteful.[86] The noise and smell of firearms tended to scatter the game whereas the silent crossbow could be fired on unsuspecting animals with deadly aim.

While the deer were plentiful in Virginia and reportedly seen by the

Figure 39. One method of hunting deer that the Indians employed required that they disguise themselves in deer-skins and creep within close range of the animals

40

colonists running in herds of up to 200 head, Strachey records that there were only "some fewe . . . in our Island about Iames-towne." According to him, the deer were mostly concentrated 'towards the heads of the Rivers, though not so many amongst the Rivers."[87] The Jamestown residents, therefore, would have to wander far afield to capture deer. It would require a lot of effort under dangerous circumstances to achieve even minimal success. It was, therefore, much easier to rely on the Indian trade for venison.

To hunt deer, the Indians used two methods that reflected the short-range power of their weapons. If hunting alone, Indians camouflaged themselves in deerskin and got as close to their prey as possible by "creeping on the ground from one tree to another." Once the deer was shot, the hunter pursued it through the forest until it collapsed from loss of blood.

Colonist Henry Spelman, who lived with the Indians for over a year, describes their other method of hunting. He claims that the Indians would encircle a herd of deer and set fire to the grass. The panicking deer, finding no way to escape the burning grasses, were drawn into a tighter and tighter circle until they were within easy range of the Indians' bows.

Native American Pottery

An unexpected indication of Indian involvement in the exchange of goods is found in the Indian pottery excavated from James Fort. The excavations have uncovered over 11,000 sherds of Indian-made pottery from colonial contexts. The majority is a Late Woodland type known as Roanoke ware,[88] named after the island in North Carolina where it was first defined in the 1940s by National Park Service archaeologist J.C. Harrington. The Indian ware was found mixed with European artifacts in a late 16th-century ditch of the English settlement of Fort Raleigh.[89] Roanoke ware is known widely in the outer Coastal Plain of southeastern Virginia and northeastern North Carolina,[90] and is the type of pottery produced by the Pasbeheghs, the nearest Indian group to the Jamestown colony.[91]

The clay used in Roanoke ware is tempered with bits of shell to make it stronger and to reduce cracking when it is fired. Its only decoration is simple stamping, which is sometimes

Figure 40. Rim section from a large Roanoke ware pot from Pit 1. Inset shows detail of simple-stamped surface treatment created by a fiber-wrapped paddle.

Figure 41. Rim section from a Potomac Creek pot found in the bulwark trench.

obscured when the surface of the vessel[92] is smoothed. Simple-stamping consists of overlapped impressions from a fiber-wrapped paddle, which, unlike cord-marked pottery, yields a pattern with crisp, straight edges. The stamping not only resulted in a decorative pot, but it also served to bind the hand-coiled pot together.

Analyses of the temper, inclusions that are in the clay which are either added purposely or occur naturally, and the surface treatment have been completed for the Indian pottery from Pit 1 within James Fort. This is a sprawling 20-ft. by 16-ft. feature consisting of five sub-pits, some of which were probably dug by the colonists for daub. It appears to have been filled no later than 1610. Nearly all, 95 percent, of the 736 sherds of Indian pottery, which could be typed within this feature, were tempered with shell. Over half, 55 percent, were both shell-tempered and simple-stamped.

Among the Roanoke ware are many sizeable sherds, some mending together, that appear to be part of one large fire-blackened cooking pot. The stamping has been applied in a diagonal orientation from the straight rim, which is at least 32 cm in diameter. From the number of large sherds that mend together, the pot appears to have been broken shortly before it was thrown away and, thus, represents the earliest-known instance of European use and discard of a Native American vessel.[93]

Another example of the colonists using Indian pottery can be seen in the bulwark trench surrounding the Fort. This pottery occurs in the earliest sequence of trench fill, which dates to ca.1610 based on the artifacts and the butchered remains of horses. Traditionally a taboo food, horsemeat was eaten by desperate colonists during the Starving Time of 1609-1610.[94]

The pot in the bulwark trench, represented by several large sherds, is interesting because it is a non-local ware type known as Potomac Creek, and it has obvious residues from cooked foods.

Potomac Creek ware was first named by American archaeologist William Henry Holmes in 1903 after the site upon which it was found.[95] Potomac Creek was the site of Patawomeke, the major village of the Algonquian Indians by the same name where John Smith traded for foodstuffs in the summer of 1608 during his explorations of the Chesapeake Bay. The colonists maintained friendly relations with the Patawomekes in the following years and depended frequently on them for supplies of corn. Perhaps Potomac Creek is most famously known as the area from which Captain Samuel Argall kidnapped Pocahontas in 1613, with the assistance of the Patawomeke chief Japazaws and his wife.

Potomac Creek pottery has its greatest concentration in "the inner coastal plain of the Potomac River"[96] but it also has been found on sites west to the Piedmont and south into Henrico County.[97] The ware is not common in the Tidewater area, but it is not surprising to find it at James Fort, considering the important role the Patawomekes played in the native trading network, as well as in supplying the colonists. The name *Patawomeke* means *trading center*,[98] which the village became as a result of its location along "the great natural trade route of the Potomac River, connecting Chesapeake Bay and the Appalachian Mountains."[99]

Potomac Creek pottery, which is dated from ca. AD 1200 to the 17th-century, consists of small to large vessels with globular bodies and straight or everted (slightly out-turned) rims.[100] The fabric, or body of the pot, is composed of "compact, hard clay, tempered with 20 to 25 percent crushed quartz (or occasionally with other local rocks) and/or medium to fine sand grains."[101] There are two major types recognized within the ware that are

Figure 42. Pocahontas was visiting the Patawomekes when she was lured onto an English ship and held hostage by Captain Samuel Argall. Pocahontas can be seen in the left foreground between Japazaws, the Patawomeke chief, and his wife who is feigning tears as she pleads to go aboard Argall's ship. This was all a ploy to get Pocahontas onto the ship, for which the couple was rewarded with a copper kettle "and some other less valuable toys." In the background, Pocahontas can be seen getting into the ship's dinghy and then sitting down for a meal with her English hosts.

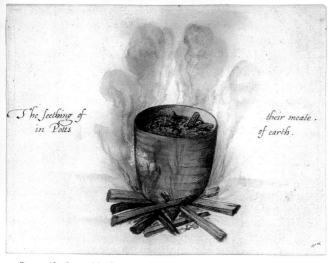

The seething of their meate in Pots of earth.

Figure 43. Painted by Roanoke Colonist John White, this round-bottomed Indian pot contains a meat/corn stew.

distinguished from each other by surface treatment: Potomac Creek Cord-Marked and Potomac Creek Plain. The vessel in the bulwark trench is the latter type, which is the most common variety in the 17th century.[102]   As on some Potomac Creek Plain vessels, the rim of the Jamestown pot has been impressed with a cord-wrapped dowel. The horizontal and diagonal markings are in a band around the rim.

The most interesting thing about the Potomac Creek pot is the cooked food residues it contains. A sherd from the pot was tested to see if these remains could be identified. The study combined techniques of gas chromatography/mass spectrometry and light stable isotope analysis to extract and ascertain the identity of any lipids contained in the sherd.[103] Lipids are the fats and fat-like compounds that occur in living organisms. When food is cooked in unglazed pottery the lipids and water-soluble compounds are absorbed into the walls of the vessel where they are protected from chemical degradation by the clay. Even when archaeologists washed the pot almost 400 years later, it wasn't enough to dislodge the absorbed lipids!

The study revealed that the Potomac Creek sherd from James Fort contained fatty acids, cholesterol and sitosterol, a plant compound. Analysis of the molecular makeup of the residue points to a C4 plant[104], which indicates corn because "maize is the only C4 plant in the eastern and midwestern United States."[105]   In addition, the presence of nitrogen in the sample suggests a small amount of meat or flesh from an animal quite low on the food chain, such as deer. Therefore, the pot from the bulwark trench, once contained a mixed stew of meat — probably deer — and corn that was cooked within the vessel. It is quite likely that the Indians brought the pot into the Fort either already containing prepared food or with the intent of cooking a meal for the colonists at the Fort. Once the contents of the vessel were consumed, the colonists would have had no use for a round-bottom cooking pot that could easily roll off their tables and would have discarded it.

There are many references in the historical records to the Indians bringing food to the colonists. At times, the meals were prepared before they arrived at the Fort, as when John Smith states that "the Indians brought us great store both of Corne and bread ready made."[106]   These foodstuffs may have been brought in the pots that had been used to cook them. The pots were then left with the colonists rather than carried out again.

But there could be another explanation for Indian pottery usage within James Fort. While it was not widely publicized to the investors back in England, the historical record indicates that there were Indians living in the Fort and working for the colonists. One Indian, whom the colonists called Kempes, lived at Jamestown for almost a year before dying of scurvy in 1610[107]. While living amongst the colonists, he learned to speak English and attended daily church services. Even his name was probably bestowed upon him by his new English "family" for the word *kemp* is an old English word meaning "brave strong warrior."[108] Another Indian, named Machumps, is recorded to have said the grace before the meal "at Sir Thos. Dale's table."[109] Further, until Captain Yeardley returned to England in 1617, he is known to have kept an Indian to shoot fowl for him and that "divers other had Salvages in like manner for their men." In the words of the colonists: "thus we lived together as if wee had beene one people."[110]

While this is only referring to "men," it is very likely, with the scarcity of women colonists in the first few years, that female Indians also were a common sight about the Fort. This is especially likely since women were responsible for preparing food in the Powhatan society and, as stated earlier, food comprised the Indians' most valuable means for barter with the English. With all these women coming in contact with the mostly male colonists, it is only natural that there would be some fraternization between the two groups. To some extent, both sides encouraged it. The colonists were instructed to cultivate the goodwill of the native peoples, and Powhatan, perceiving the gender imbalance in the fledgling colony, often offered tribal women to the colonists. This was nothing unusual to the Virginia natives. Women were customarily exchanged to create bonds of friendship and to gain allies within the Indian society. Powhatan built his chiefdom by using marriage to create alliances among the many small tribal groups in his territory.[111]

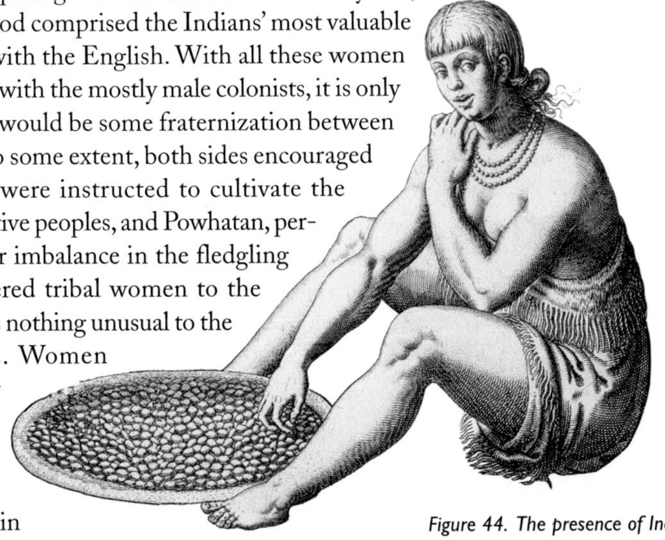

Figure 44. The presence of Indian women in and about the Fort may have been more common than the historical records have indicated.

Besides the famous marriage of John Rolfe and Pocahontas in 1614, there are very few references to the English taking Indian brides. When such an occurrence is mentioned, it is usually noted that the woman has been Christianized. Such is the case in the 1638 marriage of a Nansemond Indian woman and the son of a member of the

45

House of Burgesses. Not recorded in any extant official document but inscribed in a family-owned 17th-century book of sermons, is the record of marriage of Elizabeth, the baptized Christian daughter of the King of the Nansemond Nation, and John Bass.[112] This union marks the beginning of the Christianized Nansemond Indians of Virginia, and yet it is known only through private family documents. How common were these Indian-white marriages and how many have been undocumented?

On one occasion, the officials of the Virginia Company promoted intermarriage as a means to get rid of a financial burden, but couched the act as a way to spread Christianity to the Virginia natives. In 1621, they sent two "Virginian virgins" to Bermuda to be married to "honest English husbands."[113] These women had accompanied Pocahontas to London in 1616 and had been living there, on the company dole, ever since. To "free the Company of the weeklie charge" for keeping the "two Indian Maydes"[114] the decision was made to send them off to Bermuda to be married "to as fitt and agreeable an husband as the place could afford."[115] The deal was sweetened with servants and supplies. Only one "Virginian mayde" survived the sea voyage to be married in a "fasionable and full manner" which included over a hundred guests and "all sortes of prouisions that the Ilands could afford in a very plentiful manner." The plan was for the couple to eventually return to Virginia and thereby serve as an example to the Indian society. Through the generosity and goodwill demonstrated by the English colonists, it was hoped that the woman's relatives in Virginia, especially her brother who had succeeded as chief,[116] would "be encouraged both to continue and augment ther former freindshyp, and to become Christians themselves."[117]

A letter from Don Pedro de Zuòiga, the Spanish ambassador to London, written to the King of Spain, suggests that by 1612 there were 40 or 50 intermarriages between the English and the Indians. These alliances do not appear to have been officially condoned by the church as Zuòiga relates that "a zealous minister of (the colonists') sect was seriously wounded in many places"[118] because

Figure 45. After the successful marriage of John Rolfe and Pocahontas, the governor of Virginia, Sir Thomas Dale sent Ralph Hamor to barter for Powhatan's youngest daughter on his behalf. The mission was not successful.

he reproached the men for this practice.

But were all the "marriages" really marriages or informal liaisons? The same year that Rolfe and Pocahontas were married, the governor of the colony, Sir Thomas Dale, decided that he too should have an Indian "bride." This decision was made despite the fact that he already had a wife in England who he had married in 1611,

Figure 46. The colonists record that the Indians often presented them with bows and arrows when they participated in gift exchange.

and to whom he would return within two years! Dale's quarry was Powhatan's youngest daughter, age 12, and he sent Ralph Hamor to the chief to plead his case. On behalf of Dale, Hamor offered three times the original bride price, including beads, copper, hatchets, knives, wooden combs, fishhooks, and a grinding stone, to make Powhatan's daughter "his neerest companion, wife, and bedfellow."[119] Powhatan refused, so it will never be known how Dale planned to sanctify the marriage. Surely the ministers in the colony would never officiate over a union they knew to be bigamous!

Official unions or not, if there were a number of Indian-Colonist couples living in and around the Fort, it would make sense that there would be Indian women preparing food in their customary manner. But while this may help to explain the presence in the colonial contexts of the Roanoke ware cooking pots, which were produced by the local Indian groups, it does not clarify the occurrence of Potomac Creek pottery made over 100 miles away. Perhaps the presence of this ware is more the result of traditional aboriginal exchange, which served not only to distribute goods over wide areas but also to cement bonds between the different Indian groups.[120] It is known from the records that the Powhatan traded materials with the Patowomekes, for at the time Pocahontas was kidnapped she was at the Patowomeke village "to exchange some of her fathers commodities for theirs."[121] There is no reason why pottery could not be part of this exchange of goods. Even a Jamestown colonist thought the Indian pots "of our ordinary earth" exotic enough to send four back to England as gifts in 1608.[122]

A Potomac Creek vessel would be different, and thereby something special, to a member of a group making shell-tempered wares. As a somewhat prized pot, it may have been chosen by the Powhatans from their retinue of vessels as an appropriate container in which to carry food to the colonists for a special feast.

Projectile Points

Historical records also mention that the Indians presented arrows to the colonists, and it is possible that the remains of some of these have been recovered in the excavations at Jamestown. The Indians made arrows "of straight young sprigs which they head with bone, some 2 or 3 inches long. These they vse to shoot at squirrels on trees." Other arrows were made of reeds. These are "peeced with wood" and "headed with splinters of christall or some sharpe stone."[123]

On John Smith's 1608 exploration of the Chesapeake Bay, he was presented with "venison, beares flesh, fish, bowes, arrows, clubs, targets, and beareskins" by the Massawomeck Indians. On the same trip the Susquesahanock Indians "came downe with presents of venison, Tobacco pipes, Baskets, Targets, Bowes and Arrows"[124] and an Indian delivered "a Quiver of Arrowes" to Smith "as a present."[125] Could some of the arrowheads that have been found in and around the Fort site possibly be the result of these gifts?

A study of the stone heads of arrows, called hafted bifaces by archaeologists, which had been recovered from the James Fort excavations between 1994 and 1998,[126] recorded the shape and material of the points to determine date and origin. The artifacts also were examined for breakage patterns that might reveal function.

About half of the sample included triangular bifaces which colonist Strachey described as being "in the form of a heart barbed and jagged,"[127] that were dated to the time of contact. The other half was comprised of other types of arrowheads that represented earlier occupations at the site ranging from the Late Archaic (4000 B.C.) to the Middle Woodland (900 A.D.). Since size has the potential for indicating function, the triangular points were further separated into two groups measuring over or less than 3.3 cm in length. The smaller triangular bifaces are probably true points for arrows whereas the larger ones are more likely cutting tools.

Nine different lithic materials were recorded for the triangular points. Locally available quartzite and quartz are the most common materials for both sizes, comprising 79% of all the triangular points. This is hardly surprising, nor is the metavolcanic material, also found locally, which was used for one small triangular point. But the other raw materials re-

Figure 47. Non-local triangular projectile points from James Fort.

corded in the assemblage — jasper, dark chert, and orthoquartzite — are "extremely rare if not altogether absent in local gravels."[128]   The closest sources for these lithics are the outer Coastal Plain (Eastern Shore and Virginia Beach) for jasper, the mountainous Appalachians for dark chert, and northeastern North Carolina for orthoquartzite.[129]

Examination of the breakage patterns on the small triangular points produced some interesting results relative to function. Researchers noted that "the small triangular points made of jasper and dark chert, both non-local materials, have been recovered intact significantly more often (47 percent) than those made of other materials (11 percent)."[130]   This could be an indication that these higher quality non-local points were not intended as ordinary projectiles but were given special treatment. Rather than representing arrows that had been fired into the Fort during times of Anglo-Indian unrest, they may have found their way into colonial contexts as gift arrows. This is an area of study that will be pursued in the future. Specifically, patterns of distribution within the excavation area will be plotted for all the Native American artifacts to see how they, and specifically hafted bifaces, relate to each other and to the early colonial material.

Clay tobacco pipes

As mentioned previously, clay tobacco pipes were also among the items offered by the Indians in trade. The early narratives describe the important role played by tobacco in native rituals, whether it was cast into the river to pacify storm-roughened waters or thrown into fire during a religious ceremony.[131]   Tobacco also appears to have played a meaningful part in the social ceremonies in the Indian culture. Ralph Hamor relates that the first thing Powhatan did when he visited him in 1614 was to offer him a "pipe of

Figure 48. Indian-made tubular clay pipe from Structure 165.

Tobacco whereof himself first drank and then gave to me. And when I had drank what I pleased I returned his pipe."[132]   The pipe of tobacco as a symbol of friendship was graphically demonstrated to the colonists on one of their first encounters with native peoples after arriving in May 1607. At the village of the Appomattox they encountered a chief "with his Arrow readie in his bow in one hand, and taking a Pipe of Tobacco in the other." Although they could not understand what the man was saying, the English clearly understood the choice they were being offered and "made signes of peace."[133]

George Percy, who is the author of this account, described the pipe that was offered to him during one smoking session with the Indians. It was

Figure 49. Pipe bowl made out of the local clay in the form of a bridled horse.

"made artificially of earthe as ours are, but far bigger, with the bowle fashioned together with a piece of fine copper."[134] The addition of copper to the bowl may signify a special ceremonial pipe, as these are not represented among the large number of Indian-made tobacco pipes in the Virginia archaeological record.

Two native-made tubular clay tobacco pipes have been excavated during the Jamestown Rediscovery Project that may indicate gifts from the Indians. As Percy had observed, the bowls of these pipes are much bigger than the small pear-shaped white ball clay pipes that were made in early 17th-century London. The English bowls are thought to have been small because tobacco was rather expensive and most individuals could not afford to fill an Indian-sized bowl with tobacco. But the capacity of the bowl may also relate to the strength of the tobacco that was being smoked. The *nicotiana rustica* that the Virginia Indians were growing was very strong and, as one colonist described it, "bearing a byting tast."[135] Perhaps a couple of drafts of it were all one could comfortably manage. "The fuming vapor of tobacco," noted one early 17th-century author, "will cause some to be drunke & to have a reeling giddiness in their heads"[136] The Indians' use of larger bowls may relate to their greater tolerance of the weed or, more likely, to their attitude towards the function of the to-bacco pipe. They may not have viewed pipes as personal possessions but as instruments to be shared during the social activity of smoking, thereby necessitating the need for a large enough bowl to allow a number of individuals to partake.

While these tubular pipes are typical Late Woodland Algonquian examples, there is another locally made pipe bowl from the same context within the Fort that is an anomaly. It is a hand-molded and burnished effigy pipe. There are only two other locally made pipes with sculptured imagery known from colonial contexts in the Chesapeake. One is a sala-mander effigy from a ca. 1635-45 site in Newport News, Virginia,[137] and the other is a human effigy from Pope's Fort in St. Mary's City, Maryland. The latter is from a ca. 1645-55 context and bears an ornate rouletted design.[138]

The pipe from Jamestown consists of the bowl only. The top of the bowl has been flattened and an ear has been pulled up above the rim on each side. On the front of the bowl, facing the smoker, simple incised lines a face with two almond-shaped eyes, a band at the forehead and around the chin line, and two bands down the nose. A small hole has been punched on either side of the face but they do not penetrate the interior wall of the bowl. So the purpose of the holes was not for the effect of having smoke

Figure 50. Elements of a saddle including the iron bracing and stirrups. This saddle as well as many other elements of horse equipment were thrown away after the horses were eaten during the "Starving Time" winter of 1609-1610.

pouring from the ears but rather as a means of hanging the pipe around one's neck or possibly for suspension of a "bridle." It has been suggested that the effigy is representing a bridled horse[139] and, indeed, there is an additional pad of clay that has been added to the back of the bowl as if to represent the arch of a horse's neck.

Prior to the 1610 seal date of this context, there were several horses at Jamestown. After leaving London in May 1609, the 3rd Supply stopped at Plymouth on the west coast of England for the express purpose of picking up horses. Colonist Gabriel Archer records that "six Mares and two Horses" were loaded into *The Blessing*, which was the ship upon which he also traveled.[140] John Smith remarks that when he left in the fall of 1609 there were "six Mares and a Horse,"[141] which became sustenance for the starving colonists over the following winter. This is probably the first time the Powhatans had seen horses, and Smith records that they were in great awe of these animals, just as they were of lightning, thunder and the colonists' firearms and artillery power. The Indians worshiped horses as they did "all things that were able to do them hurt beyond their prevention."[142] It makes sense that they would use the image of something feared on a tobacco pipe, since tobacco was such an important part of their rituals to placate evil forces.

Tenter Hooks

Another type of artifact that has been found in the Fort excavations was not directly traded between the colonists and the Indians, but it may represent goods that were. These artifacts are small L-shaped hooks known as tenter hooks. Randle Holme, 17th-century chronicler of material culture, states that "the Tentry hook, is a nail with a crooked head, yet sharp pointed, that it may strike into any thing hung upon it."[143] In England, tenter hooks were used primarily by the textile industry to stretch cloth as it was drying. Cloth, particularly wool, required washing and fulling (or thickening) as part of the finishing process. "Fulling not only mats the

Figure 52. Iron tenter hooks possibly used for stretching the hides of animals obtained in trade by the colonists.

fabric, but shrinks it considerably too."[144] The fabric was hung up for drying on wooden tenters which "consisted of a line of posts with housings to support horizontal rails. Pairs of rails, each with a row of tenter hooks, were set between the posts, the hooks in the upper rail pointing upwards, and in the lower rail downwards, thus enabling the tension of attached cloth to be adjusted."[145]

It is not considered that the colonists were involved in producing cloth at Jamestown. The lucrative textile industry was highly regulated in England and competition from the colonies would not have been tolerated by those involved. It is probably for this reason that the Virginia Company did not send sheep — from which wool and thereby cloth could be derived — among the domestic animals. Instead, the 40 tenter hooks that have been excavated so far, were probably being used to stretch and dry animal skins that the colonists received in trade from the Indians. Furs were a welcome commodity in London, and the colonists were encouraged to trade for them. One 1610 attempt by the Virginia

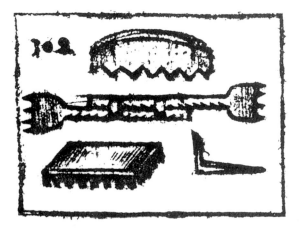

Figure 53. Seventeenth-century drawing of a tenter hook.

Company to guide the colonists towards lucrative exports listed "beaver skins being taken in wintertime will yield good profit; the like will otter skins."[146] The mariners dropping off the colonists at Jamestown realized the marketability of the country's animal skins and would trade illegally for "otter skins, beavers, rokoone furs, bears skins, etc."[147] One sailor reputedly sold £30 worth of furs in England at a time when the colony had acquired none.[148] This black-market dealing totally upset the colonists' balance of trade with the Indians by overvaluing the native goods which, in turn, contributed to the demise of the already crumbling intercultural relationship.

Endnotes

[1] William M. Kelso, *Jamestown Rediscovery Archaeological Project:* "The Search for the Site of James Fort (1607) at Jamestown," (Richmond, Virginia: Association for the Preservation of Virginia Antiquites, 1993), 5.

[2] Richard Randolph, "Island of Jamestown," *Southern Literary Messenger, III*: 1837, 303-304; John L. Cotter, *Archaeological Excavations at Jamestown* (Washington, District of Colombia: National Park Service, United States Department of Interior, 1958), 3-6.

[3] William M. Kelso, et al., *Jamestown Rediscovery, I-VI*, (Richmond, Virginia: APVA, 1995-2000).

[4] Douglas Owsley, "Immigrants and Residents: Isotope Signatures in the Chesapeake During the Colonial Period," (paper presented at Human Remains: Conservation, Retrieval and Analysis Conference, Williamsburg, Virginia, November 1999).

[5] Dr. Paul Budd, personal communication, University of Bradford, 1999.

[6] Julian Litten, *The English Way of Death*, (London: Robert Hale Limited, 1992), 99.

[7] Owsley, op cit.

[8] Phillip L. Barbour, ed. *The Complete Works of Captain John Smith (1580 -1631)* (Chapel Hill, North Carolina: The University of North Carolina Press, 1986), II: 235-236; William Strachey, "A True Reportory of the Wreck and Redemption of Sir Thomas Gates, Knight," in *A Voyage to Virginia in 1609*, ed. Louis B. Wright (Charlottesville, Virginia: University Press of Virginia, 1964), 80-82.

[9] Barbour, III: 216.

[10] Strachey, *True Reportory*, 81.

[11] Ibid.

[12] William M. Kelso, Nicholas Luccketti, and Beverly Straube, *Jamestown Rediscovery IV*, (Richmond, Virginia: APVA, 1998), 33-35.

[13] Barbour, *John Smith*, II: 180-181.

[14] Strachey, *True Reportory*, 64.

[15] Kelso, et al., *Jamestown Rediscovery IV*: 33.

[16] This analysis was done in 1997 by Beta Analytic Inc.

[17] Gary Parks, ed., *Virginia Land Records*, (Baltimore, Maryland: Geneological Publishing Co., 1982), 253.

[18] Samuel H. Yonge, *The Site of Old Jamestown* (Richmond, Virginia: APVA, 1903), 78; Martha W. McCartney, *James City County, Keystone of the Commonwealth*, (Virginia Beach, Virginia: The Donning Company, 1997), 80.

[19] Yonge, 78-97.

[20] Peter Force, *Tracts and Other Papers, Relating Principally to the Original Settlement, and Progress of the Colonies in North America*, (Washington, Distric of Colombia, 1886), I: 5-24.

[21] Kelso, et al., *Jamestown Rediscovery IV*: 27.

[22] Barbour, II: 350.

[23] William M. Kelso and Beverly Straube, *Jamestown Rediscovery VI*, (Richmond, Virginia: APVA,

2000), 18.

[24] Alain Outlaw, *Governors Land: Archaeology of an Early 17th Century Virginia Settlement*, (Charlottesville, Virginia: University of Virginia Press 1990), 14-28.

[25] F.W.B. Charles, "Post Construction and the Rafter Roof", *The Vernacular Architecture Group*, Vol. VI: XII (1981), 5-8.

[26] Arber, 957.

[27] Kelso and Straube, *Jamestown Rediscovery VI*: 16.

[28] William M. Kelso, Nicholas Luccketti and Beverly Straube, *Jamestown Rediscovery V* (Richmond, Virginia: APVA, 1999), 3.

[29] Eric Mercer, English Vernacular Houses, *Her Majesties Stationary Office* (975), 1-62.

[30] Ralph Merrifield, *The Archaeology of Ritual and Magic*, (New York: New Amsterdam Books, 1987), 163-75.

[31] Robert Blair St George, *Conversing in Signs* (University of North Carolina Press, 1998), 192.

[32] Strachey, *A True Reportory*, 81-82.

[33] Dell Upton, "Early Vernacular Architecture in Southeastern Virginia," (PhD dissertation, Brown University, 1979), 28.

[34] Ian Lancashire, *Early Modern English Dictionary Database*, Department of English, University of Toronto. www. chass. utoronto. ca/english/emed/emedd.html.

[35] William Fitzhugh, *Archaeology of Kodlunarn Island in Archaeology of the Frobisher Voyages* ed. William Fitzhugh and Jaqueline Olin (Washington, Distric of Colombia: Smithsonian Institute Press), 72.

[36] Jeffrey P. Brain, 2000 excavations at the Site of Popham Colony, Peabody Museum, 2000, 10-13.

[37] Leon Cranmer, *Cushnoc: The History and Archaeology of Plymouth Fur Traders on the Kennebec*, (Occasional Publications in Maine Archaeology #7, Maine Historical Society, 1990), 57.

[38] Rodney Cousins, *Lincolnshire Buildings in the Mud and Stud Tradition*, (Lincoln, Heritage Lincolnshire 2000), 7-9; Keith Miller, "The Survey of a Lincolnshire Vernacular Farmhouse," in *Land People and Landscapes: Essays on the History of the Lincolnshire Region* ed. by Dinah Tyszka, Keith Miller and Geoffrey Bryant, eds., Lincolnshire County Council, 1991), 77.

[39] Rodney Cousins, personal communication, 2001.

[40] Parish christening records from the Lincoln record office on Family Search Geneology website www.familysearch.org.

[41] A database of biographical information in development by Catherine Correll-Walls, APVA.

[42] Edmund S. Morgan, *The Puritan Dilemma*, (Boston, Massachusetts: Little Brown and Co., ed., 1958), 18-34.

[43] Further research is clearly needed to look at these existing structures to better discern whether the similarities present on the surface will hold up to a rigorous comparison of the architectural and archaeological remains of the two regions

[44] M.W. Barley, *The English Farmhouse and Cottage* (London: Routlage and Kegan Paul 1961), 57-58.

[45] Beverly Straube and Nicholas Luccketti, *1995 Interim Report on the APVA Excavations at Jamestown, Virginia* (Richmond, Virginia: APVA 1996), 10.

[46] James Deetz, *In Small Things Forgotten* (New York: Anchor Books, 1996), 172.

[47] Nicholas Luccketti and Beverly Straube, *1997 Interim Report on the APVA Excavations at Jamestown, Virginia* (Richmond, Virginia: APVA, 1998), 4.

[48] Barbour, I: 233, II: 325.

[49] Barbour, I: 61.

[50] Strachey, *A True Reportory* , 79.

[51] Barbour, III: 276.

[52] Barbour, I: 172.

[53] Barbour, I: 169.

[54] Barbour, I: 59.

[55] David Quinn, *The Roanoke Voyages, 1584-1590* (London: The Hakluyt Society, 1955), 101.

[56] Seth Mallios, *In the Hands of "Indian Givers": Exchange and Violence at Ajacan, Roanoke, and Jamestown*, (Ph.D. dissertation, University of Virginia, 1998), 71-74.

[57] Artifact types quantified by weight instead of count—like brick, slag, cullet, etc.—are not included in the calculation.

[58] The value should be entered as a decimal value. If 5% of an assemblage is copper, (x) is .05.

[59] Seth Mallios and Beverly Straube, *1999 Interim Report on the APVA Excavations at Jamestown, Virginia* (Richmond, Virginia: APVA, 2000), 26.

[60] Seth Mallios and Garrett Fesler, *Archaeological Excavations at 44JC568, the Reverend Richard Buck Site* (Richmond, Virginia: APVA, 1999).

[61] Seth Mallios, *At the Edge of the Precipice: Frontier Ventures, Jamestown's Hinterland, and the Archaeology of 44JC802* (Richmond, Virginia: APVA, 2000).

[62] Barbour, I: 215.

[63] Mallios, *Indian Givers*, 202-292; Stephen Potter, "Early English Effects on Virginia Algonquian Exchange and Tribute in the Tidewater Potomac," in *Powhatan's Mantle*, Peter Wood, Gregory A. Waselkov, and M. Thomas Hatley, eds., (Lincoln, Nebraska: University of Nebraska Press, 1989), 157.

[64] Greek philosopher Aristotle was the first to record a variant of this proverb. In ca. 350BC, he wrote in *Elenchi* that, "Yellow-colored objects appear to be gold." Many others have altered the saying, including Shakespeare, who wrote in *The Merchant of Venice* (2. 7. 65) that, "All that glisters is not gold."

[65] Barbour, II: 157.

[66] Straube and Luccketti, *1995 Interim Report;* Luccketti and Straube, *1997 Interim Report.*

[67] Barbour, II: 121.

[68] See discussion in William Kelso and Beverly Straube, *Jamestown Rediscovery VI.* (The Association for the Preservation of Virginia Antiquities, 2000), 33-35.

[69] Barbour, II: 206.

[70] "Corn" in America indicates maize, but in England it is any cereal including wheat, oats, and

barley.

[71] Kathleen Brown, *Good Wives, Nasty Wenches, and Anxious Patriarchs* (Chapel Hill, North Carolina: University of North Carolina Press, 1996), 46.

[72] Barbour, II: 112.

[73] Ibid.; William Strachey, *The Historie of Travell Into Virginia Britania (1612)*, Louis B. Wright and Virginia Freund, eds., (London, Hakluyt Society, 1953), 118.

[74] Strachey, op cit., 81.

[75] A pottage is a thick soup.

[76] C. Anne Wilson, *Food and Drink in Britain* (Harper & Row Publishers, Inc., 1974), 210-212.

[77] Barbour, II: 205.

[78] Barbour, I: 212.

[79] Joanne Bowen and Susan Trevarthen Andrews, "The Starving Time at Jamestown," (Report Submitted to the Association for the Preservation of Virginia Antiquities, 2000), 2.

[80] Barbour, II: 199.

[81] Strachey, *The Historie of Travell*, 83.

[82] Howard L. Blackmore, *Hunting Weapons from the Middle Ages to the Twentieth Century*.1971 Reprint. (Mineola, New York: Dover Publications, Inc., 2000), 291.

[83] Strachey, *The Historie of Travell*, 126.

[84] Barbour, *John Smith*, II: 194.

[85] Roger B. Manning, *Hunters and Poachers* (Oxford: Clarendon Press, 1993), 7.

[86] Blackmore, 155.

[87] Strachey, 124.

[88] E. Randolph Turner of the Virginia Department of Historic Resources is kindly doing this analysis for the APVA Jamestown Rediscovery Project.

[89] J. C. Harrington, "Plain Stamped, Shell Tempered Pottery from North Carolina," *American Antiquity* 13:3 (1948), 251.

[90] Margaret C. Blaker, "Further Comments on Simple-Stamped Shell-Tempered Pottery," *American Antiquity* 17: 3 (1952), 257-258.

[91] Traditionally the ware has been dated ca.1500-1625, although radiocarbon dates from the recently reported Great Neck Site in Virginia Beach, Virginia (VB7) suggest an even earlier beginning date in the 15th century. Mary Ellen Norrisey Hodges, "Native American Settlement at Great Neck: Report on VDHR Archaeological Investigations of Woodland Components at Site 44VB7, Virginia Beach, Virgnina, 1981-1987," Virginia Department of Historic Resources Research Report Series 9 (Richmond, Virginia: VDHR, 1998).

[92] Dennis Blanton, personal communication, 1994.

[93] E. Randolph Turner, personal communication, 1995.

[94] Bowen and Andrews, 75.

[95] David J. Meltzer and Robert C. Dunnell, eds., *The Archaeology of William Henry Holmes* (Washington: Smithsonian Institution Press, 1992), 155.

[96] Stephen R. Potter, *Commoners, Tribute, and Chiefs: the Development of Algonquian Culture in the Potomac Valley*.(Charlottesville, Virginia: University of Virginia Press, 1993), 125.

[97] Potomac Creek ware has been

noted in Henrico, Goochland, and Orange counties (Jeffrey L. Hantman, personal communication, 2000).

[98] Phillip L. Barbour, "The Earliest Reconnaissance of the Chesapeake Bay Area," *The Virginia Magazine of History and Biography* 79:3 (July 1971), 296.

[99] Potter, 160.

[100] Ibid., 125.

[101] Ibid., 123.

[102] Keith T. Egloff and Stephen R. Potter, "Indian Ceramics from Coastal Plain Virginia," *Archaeology of Eastern North America.* Volume 10 (Fall 1982), 112.

[103] Eleanora A. Reber, Report on a Preliminary Project of the Identification of Maize in Absorbed Pottery Residues from Sites throughout the New World. (Harvard University. Unpublished ms. on file Jamestown Rediscovery Center, The Association for the Preservation of Virginia Antiquities, 1999).

[104] Plants have one of three pathways of carbon dioxide respiration: C3, C4, and CAM. CAM plants are succulents and cacti, C4 plants include all the tropical grasses, and the rest are C3 plants, which are adapted to temperate climates. Corn is a tropical grass that required considerable adaptation to thrive in eastern and mid western North America (Reber: 13).

[105] Ibid., 13.

[106] Barbour, I: 35.

[107] Strachey, *The Historie of Travell*, 61.

[108] *Compact Oxford English Dictionary* (Oxford: Clarendon Press, 1998), 911: 383.

[109] Strachey, *The Historie of Travell*, 98.

[110] Barbour, II: 257.

[111] Powhatan, according to Henry Spelman, had a pattern of selecting the "fairest and comeliest maids" from "all parts of the country" as his wives. If a wife has a child, she is returned to her people "with sufficient copper and beads to maintain her and the child while it is young" [Henry Spelman "Relation of Virginia, 1609," in *Jamestown Narratives, Eyewitness Accounts of the Virginia Colony*, Edward Wright Haile ed. (Champlain, Virginia: Round House Publishing, 1998), 488-489.]. Powhatan thereby creates a familial alliance with every tribal group from which he selects a bride.

[112] Documentation held by the Nansemond Indian Tribal Association. Thanks to Dinah Everett, curator of the Isle of Wight County Museum, for sharing this information with the author.

[113] General Sir J. Henry Lefroy, ed., *The Historye of the Bermudaes or Summer Islands Attributed to Captain Nathaniel Butler.* (London: Hakluyt Society, 1st Ser., LXV, 1882), 271.

[114] Susan M. Kingsbury, *Records of the Virgnia Company* (Washington, District of Colombia: Government Printing Office, 1906), 485.

[115] Lefroy, 284.

[116] Is this Powhatan's brother, Opitchapham? This would make the "Indian mayde" Pocahontas' aunt.

[117] Lefroy, 284.

[118] Alexander Brown, *The Genesis of the United States* (Cambridge: The Riverside Press, 1891), 572.

[119] RalphHamor, A True Discourse of the Present State of Virginia. Reprint of 1615 edition. (Richmond, Virginia: The Virginia State Library, 1957), 41

[120] James H. Merrel, "Our Bond of Peace": Patterns of Intercultural Exchange in the Carolina Piedmont, 1650-1750," *Powhatan's Mantle*. Peter H. Wood et al. eds., (University of Nebraska Press, 1989), 198.

[121] Hamor, 4.

[122] Phillip L. Barbour, *The Jamestown Voyages Under the First Charter, 607-1609* (Cambridge: The University Press, 1969), 161.

[123] Barbour, *Jamestown Voyages*, 357.

[124] Barbour, I: 231.

[125] Barbour, II: 177.

[126] Dennis B. Blanton et al., "Brief and True Report of Projectile Points from Jamestown Rediscovery contexts as of December 1998." (Report for the Association for the Preservation of Virginia Antiquities, 1999).

[127] Strachey, 109.

[128] Blanton, 1.

[129] Ibid.

[130] Ibid, 2.

[131] Barbour, I: 59; Barbour, II: 124.

[132] Hamor: 39-40.

[133] Barbour, *Jamestown Voyages*, 138.

[134] Ibid, 136.

[135] Strachey, *The Historie of Travell*, 123.

[136] Edmund Gardiner (1611) *Phisicall and Approved Medicines.*

The English Experience Number 191, (New York: Dà Capo Press, 1969), 53.

[137] The Boldrop Site, 44NN40; collection on file with Jamestown Rediscovery Center.

[138] Henry Miller, *Discovering Maryland's First City: a Summary Report on the 1981-1984 Archaeological Excavations in St. Mary's City, Maryland.* St. Mary's City Archaeology Series No. 2, (1986), 66.

[139] Dennis Blanton, William and Mary Archaeological Research Center, made this suggestion.

[140] Barbour, *Jamestown Voyages*, 278.

[141] Barbour, II: 326.

[142] Barbour, I: 169.

[143] Randle Holme, *The Academy of Armory and Blazon*, (Chester: Printed for the Author, 1688), III: 348.

[144] Penelope Walton "Textiles," in *English Medieval Industry*, John Blair and Nigel Ramsey, eds. (London: The Hambledon Press, 1991), 332.

[145] Ian H. Goodall, "Iron textile manufacturing tools," *Norwich Households*, Sue Margeson, ed., East Anglian Archaeology No. 58, (1993), 182.

[146] Virginia Company of London, "Instructions for such things as are to be sente from Virginia 1610," in Alexander Brown, *The Genesis of the United States* (Cambridge: The Riverside Press, 1891), 385.

[147] Strachey, *A True Reportory*, 72.

[148] Barbour, I: 240.